DOCTOR STRANGE
A DECADE OF DARK MAGIC

AN EXPLORATION BY

STUART MOORE

BLOOMSBURY ACADEMIC

NEW YORK • LONDON • OXFORD • NEW DELHI • SYDNEY

BLOOMSBURY ACADEMIC

Bloomsbury Publishing Inc, 1359 Broadway, New York, NY 10018, USA
Bloomsbury Publishing Plc, 50 Bedford Square, London, WC1B 3DP, UK
Bloomsbury Publishing Ireland, 29 Earlsfort Terrace, Dublin 2, D02 AY28, Ireland

BLOOMSBURY, BLOOMSBURY ACADEMIC and the Diana logo are
trademarks of Bloomsbury Publishing Plc

MARVEL PUBLISHING
Jeff Youngquist, VP, Production and Special Projects
Brian Overton, Manager, Special Projects
Sarah Singer, Editor, Special Projects
Jeremy West, Manager, Licensed Publishing
Sven Larsen, VP, Licensed Publishing
David Gabriel, VP, Print & Digital Publishing
C.B. Cebulski, Editor in Chief

BLOOMSBURY ACADEMIC
Haaris Naqvi, Global Editorial Director
Leah Babb-Rosenfeld, Editorial Director
Hali Han, Assistant Editor
Ian Buck, Deputy Head of Production
Zeba Talkhani, Senior Production Editor
Ben Anslow, Senior Designer

First published in the United States of America 2025
Reprinted 2025

Cover art: Frank Brunner, Dick Giordano, and Glynis Oliver
Cover design: Ben Anslow

A catalog record for this book is available from the Library of Congress.

ISBN: PB: 979-8-7651-3754-3
       ePDF: 979-8-7651-3757-4
       eBook: 979-8-7651-3755-0

Series: Marvel Age of Comics

Typeset by RefineCatch Limited, www.refinecatch.com
Printed and bound in India

For product safety related questions contact productsafety@bloomsbury.com.

To find out more visit www.bloomsbury.com/marvel-books

MARVEL
AGE OF
COMICS

For Liz
Radiant jewel, mystical wife

"I know of struggle, Wong ... of struggle undreamt and undreamable, for the fate of everything that lives ... and I know Stephen Strange is its key factor."

CLEA OF THE DARK DIMENSION, *MARVEL PREMIERE* #9 (1973), WORDS BY STEVE ENGLEHART

"He's the ever-lovin' gearest! Far as I'm concerned, the Mods have had it! That crazy cape really comes on strong!"

ADMIRING BEATNIK WOMAN, *STRANGE TALES* #147 (1966), WORDS BY STAN LEE

CONTENTS

THE ANCIENT TOMES

Strange Tales #110, 111, 114–146

by Stan Lee and Steve Ditko

with Roy Thomas, Dennis O'Neil, and George Roussos

Strange Tales #147–168

by Stan Lee, Dennis O'Neil, Bill Everett, Roy Thomas, Marie Severin, Raymond Marais, Dan Adkins, Jim Lawrence, and George Tuska

Doctor Strange #169–183

by Roy Thomas, Gene Colan, Tom Palmer, and Dan Adkins

Selections from *The Incredible Hulk*, *Sub-Mariner*, *Marvel Feature*

by Roy Thomas, Marie Severin, Johnny Craig, Herb Trimpe, Ross Andru, Bill Everett, Don Heck, Frank Giacoia, and Sal Buscema

Marvel Premiere #3–8

by Barry Windsor-Smith, Stan Lee, Dan Adkins, Roy Thomas, Archie Goodwin, Frank Brunner, Gardner F. Fox, Sam Kweskin, Don Perlin, Sal Buscema, P. Craig Russell, Mike Esposito, Frank Giacoia, Dave Hunt, and Jim Starlin

Marvel Premiere #9–14

by Steve Englehart and Frank Brunner

with Ernie Chan, the Crusty Bunkers, and Dick Giordano

Prologue: Set Time to Swirling

We all have our secrets. A kiss stolen by moonlight; a photo in a shoebox. A homemade costume stashed on the top shelf of the closet, hidden from Aunt May's fearful, loving eyes.

I don't like to admit this, especially in print. But I …

… I was a DC kid.

I *knew* about Marvel, sure. I was vaguely aware of Captain America and the Avengers; I watched the Spider-Man cartoon and had bought some of the comics. But mostly I read DC books. Super-stuff, Bat-stuff—back then, those were still the heavy hitters of the super hero world. DC had even snagged Jack Kirby away from Marvel, giving him free rein (for a while) on a whole new line of comics.

Then, one day in high school, my friend Dave sat me down with a big pile of Marvels. Single issues, piled up in neat stacks.

"Read," he said.

And suddenly, like a Kree invasion force in the sky, there it all was. Warlock, Deathlok, Son of Satan. The Black Panther and Killraven, Warrior of the Worlds. Man-Thing and his wayward spawn, Howard the Duck. The Avengers—the Defenders! The All-New X-Men, who seemed to live in a world all their own.

And, of course, there was Doctor Strange. Specifically there was *Marvel Premiere* #9, where a new creative team took over the series. Marvel wanted me to know what a big deal this was, and—in the tradition already established by Stan Lee—they weren't subtle about it. This caption headed up page one:

Ten years ago this month, Stan Lee and Steve Ditko created DR. STRANGE, MASTER OF THE MYSTIC ARTS! Now, Steve Englehart and Frank Brunner announce the reaffirmation of comics' most extraordinary series! You are cordially invited to attend! (In other words, folks: the password has just become "KOSMIC"!)

I was *cordially invited*. At age sixteen, sitting in my friend's house on a sweltering summer day, surrounded by brightly colored comic books.

How could I refuse?

TEN YEARS AGO THIS MONTH, *STAN LEE* AND *STEVE DITKO* CREATED...

Dr. STRANGE *MASTER OF THE MYSTIC ARTS!*™

NOW, *STEVE ENGLEHART* AND *FRANK BRUNNER* ANNOUNCE THE *REAFFIRMATION* OF COMICS' MOST *EXTRAORDINARY* SERIES! YOU ARE *CORDIALLY* INVITED TO *ATTEND!*

(*IN OTHER* WORDS, FOLKS: THE *PASSWORD* HAS JUST BECOME *"KOSMIC"!*)

MY *CLOAK OF LEVITATION* HAS CARRIED ME ACROSS THE ROTTING SURFACE OF THIS ENTIRE *PLANET*--

-- AND *NOWHERE* HAVE I SEEN LIFE!

I AM *TRAPPED* UPON THIS *DEAD* SPHERE-- WITH *EARTH* LOST IN AN UNKNOWN *DIRECTION* AND AT AN UNKNOWN *DISTANCE*--

-- BUT IF I CANNOT DISCOVER *SOME* MEANS OF *ESCAPE*, THE DREAD *SHUMA-GORATH* WILL LAY WASTE TO THE *COSMOS!*

THE CRYPTS OF KAA-U!

SMILIN' *STAN* *ALSO* PRESENTS: ERNIE CHUA, INKER | JOHN COSTANZA, LETTERER | DAVID HUNT, COLORIST | ROY THOMAS, EDITOR

Marvel was like that, in those days. It was a club, an elite society for kids. An oasis of high-low culture, trashy but ambitious, mangling Shakespeare, winking and pointing at your straightlaced parents. Throwing out big concepts, philosophical ideas, while poking a stick in the eye of the idea that maybe you should be reading, I don't know, a *book* instead.

And Doctor Strange dealt with the biggest concepts of all. Case in point: For their first complete storyline, writer Englehart and artist Brunner tackled nothing less than the death and rebirth of the universe. A villain from the future called Sise-Neg (read it backwards) travels back to the beginning of time to declare himself God. Announcing that he has "set time to swirling with my travel," he plans to reshape all of history according to his own design. Only Doctor Stephen Strange, with his unique abilities and perceptions, might be able to stop him.

When the MCU's *Doctor Strange* film hit theaters in 2016, millions of people around the world learned the character's story: a brilliant surgeon brought low by an accident, who slowly learns the mystic arts and begins to see a different reality, behind and beyond our own. By the time Sise-Neg came along in 1973, comic fans had already witnessed that saga and much, much more. In reaching for the stars—creatively and philosophically—Englehart and Brunner hoped to build on the series' trippy, other-dimensional foundation. Even the writer's use of the word "Kosmic," inside those cheeky quotation marks, was a signifier; it evoked head shops, underground comix, tuning in and dropping out and searching for new roads, new ways to perceive the universe.

Which, of course, had been the idea right from the start. By 1963, Stan Lee and his collaborators had already revolutionized super hero comics by introducing new levels of interpersonal drama into the proceedings. But even among those characters, Doctor Strange was … well, a bit odd. Lee always acknowledged that the strip's initial concept had come from Ditko. At times Stan seemed almost baffled by the character, like a parent shrugging at the bohemian antics of a wayward child.

And who was Steve Ditko, anyway? Whole books have been written about this brilliant, eccentric artist, who shunned direct attention. He lived in New York City for decades, laboring alone in a midtown studio where he produced comics that reflected his singular vision, right up to his death at the age of 90.

Ditko and Lee gave birth to Doctor Strange, then handed off the child to a succession of talented writers and artists. Roy Thomas, Gene Colan, DC mainstay Gardner F. Fox, Dan Adkins, Marie Severin, and many others expanded on the series' mind-bending concepts. In this volume we'll explore the character's beginnings as an arrogant, high-priced surgeon;

the twist of fate that changes his life, setting him on the road to enlightenment; his role as guardian of Earth's dimensional realm; and his lives as a masked man and super hero team leader. Following some early success, Stephen Strange went through a rough patch, hiding his face and getting by with bit parts in the pages of *Hulk* and *Sub-Mariner*. But like an actor or rock star in a career slump, he pulled himself together eventually.

All of which brings us to the death and rebirth of the universe. And back again, in a cosmic loop worthy of a Sorcerer Supreme.

Remember Dave, who introduced me to the Marvel Universe? That summer, poring through his comic collection, led me to a lifetime of wonder and professional entanglements, some of which I'll tell you about in these pages. I moved to New York as a young adult, starting out in book publishing before I slipped into the glorious gutter of the comics world. Since then I've scripted hundreds of comics, cowritten novels with Stan Lee, and worked on both sides of the Marvel editorial desk.

I even met Steve Ditko. Once.

Dave and I are still in touch. Maybe you've got a friend like him, someone who introduced you to an enduring passion at a critical time in your life. And maybe—just maybe—that passion is Marvel comics.

If so—or if all this just makes you curious!—then sit back

and join me as, like Doctor Strange, we travel back to the beginning. All the way back to the character's creative genesis, then forward through an odyssey like that of no other comic-book hero. As Englehart and Brunner once told us: "The present lives now—and the future cries for entrance."

Or, as Lee and Ditko said: "Slowly the mists begin to clear, as a strange, startling world takes form! A world in which the impossible is believable, and the incredible is commonplace …"

1

1963–1964: The Gossamer Thread

Slowly, yes, the mists begin to clear. As your eyes adjust, you find yourself on the streets of New York's famous East Village; but not the Village of today, with its sushi bars, tattoo parlors, and high-ticket gastropubs. Not even the Village of the 1980s, when we used to drink Miller High Life at sprawling student bistros and buy our comics at a little shop on Sullivan Street, right around the corner from …

… no, not yet. We'll get there.

Right now we're going all the way back to 1963. In the spring of that year, the Beatles and Boston Strangler both roamed the land. Medgar Evers appeared on TV to promote integration, then was shot dead in front of his own home. Astronaut Gordon Cooper orbited the Earth in a capsule called *Faith*; Jet Li, Julian Lennon, and Russell T. Davies were born. After nearly two decades of searching, the Soviet Union found and identified Adolf Hitler's body.

And in the back of a marginal comic called *Strange Tales*, Stan Lee and Steve Ditko presented the five-page "Dr. Strange, Master of Black Magic!" The title character made his home "on a quiet side street in New York's colorful Greenwich Village."

By this time, Stan had situated his recently launched Marvel Universe firmly in New York City. The debut issue of *Fantastic Four* included a mention of "Central City," but by issue #4 the team's skyscraper was described as being "in the caverns of New York." Spider-Man wasn't yet identified as living in Queens, but in the first issue of his own comic, he visited the Four on foot—so clearly he lived in roughly the same, friendly, neighborhood. This sense of a shared city allowed the characters to interact casually, but the choice of New York was also a natural one. In the days before Zoom and Dropbox—or email, or FedEx—writers and artists *had* to live in or near New York. That way they could drop off work, meet with editors, and pick up their freelance checks.

Most artists hadn't seen L.A., the Grand Canyon, or the Blue Area of the moon. But they all knew what Broadway looked like.

And sometimes it looked pretty rough. Manhattan in those days barely resembled today's Disneylandish playground of the rich. A hell of a lot of factors—political, economic, and technological—have contributed to the transformation; but three innovations have utterly changed New York City over the years, made it an immeasurably nicer place to live. In no particular order:

- plastic trash cans

- ubiquitous air conditioning

- the Clean Air Act

In the spring of 1963, none of those things had come to pass. Two or three nights a week, rusty behemoths prowled the predawn streets, sanitation workers leaping from the fenders, banging hard metal cans against the trucks, then flinging them to the sidewalk with a clatter to wake the dead. In the warmer months, residents sweated and sweltered, lazing on stoops and dangling bare feet from fire escapes. "Smog alerts" would virtually shut down the city, smothering it in a thick cloud of industrial filth for days at a time.

Manhattan blazed like the skull of Dormammu in the summer, and froze like Nightmare's realm of dreams in the winter months. Artist Steve Ditko lived in that world. He had chosen it as his lifelong home after growing up in flood-plagued Johnstown, Pennsylvania, and he brought the city vividly to life every month in *The Amazing Spider-Man*, his other legendary Marvel co-creation.

"Dr. STRANGE
MASTER OF BLACK MAGIC!"

MEN CALL HIM *DR. STRANGE!*

NEVER HAVE YOU KNOWN HIS LIKE!

IT IS A GREAT PLEASURE AND PRIVILEGE FOR THE EDITORS OF *STRANGE TALES* TO PRESENT, QUIETLY AND WITHOUT FANFARE, THE FIRST OF A NEW SERIES, BASED UPON A *DIFFERENT* KIND OF SUPER-HERO---

DR. STRANGE
MASTER OF
BLACK MAGIC!

STORY:	*STAN LEE*
ART:	*STEVE DITKO*
LETTERING:	*TERRY SZENICS*

SOMEWHERE IN THE CITY, BETWEEN DARKNESS AND DAWN, A TORTURED MAN TOSSES FITFULLY IN HIS BED, VAINLY SEEKING PEACE THAT WILL NOT COME...

NO! *NO!!* GO AWAY! PLEASE-- *PLEASE GO AWAY!*

IT'S NO USE! I CAN'T SLEEP! I *DARE* NOT SLEEP! IT'S THAT SAME DREAM! EVERY NIGHT THE SAME! BUT *WHY?* WHAT CAN IT *MEAN??*

I CAN'T FIGHT IT ALONE! I NEED HELP! I'VE HEARD A NAME--- SPOKEN IN WHISPERS--- *DR. STRANGE!* HE DABBLES IN BLACK MAGIC! PERHAPS *HE* CAN HELP ME!

But in the streets and coffeehouses of the Village—the impromptu Sunday music fests—artists, poets, and musicians also saw worlds of wonder, pathways in the sky. Those realms, the eldritch dimensions that could only be revealed to a sorcerer after years of intense meditation—that world was every bit as real to Ditko as Peter Parker's skyscrapers, office buildings, and suspension bridges. Or, if it wasn't, you'd never know it from what wound up on the page.

New York was a tough city in those days. But magic lived there, too.

Sixty blocks north of the Village, the Madison Avenue office of Marvel Comics was a shadow of its former self. Ten years earlier, the company had employed dozens of creatives, filling one room each in the Empire State Building with a "bullpen" of adventure and humor artists. But in the late 1950s, a series of business setbacks had led publisher Martin Goodman to lay off most of the company's staff.

Editor Stan Lee, suffering under a distribution deal that severely limited the number of titles he could publish, made the best of a bad situation. But the company's in-house bullpen now lived only in the cheerful hype that Lee crafted to attract and excite his young readers. With his stable of talent largely furloughed, Editor Stan had to rely heavily on Writer Stan to pick up the creative slack.

In order to handle the workload, Stan often asked artists to work from loose plots, sometimes talked out only in face-to-face story conferences. A few artists, notably Ditko and Jack Kirby, rose to the occasion with stellar results, and Marvel began to garner some heat with its recent super hero launches. Standouts included *Fantastic Four* and *Spider-Man*, both of which were slowly accruing an older, more sophisticated readership.

With the line capped at eight titles a month, though, story space was at a premium. Editor Stan had to move carefully.

Still, he made room for Doctor Strange.

The first story opens with a two-thirds-page poster shot of the character, his hands already twisted into those distinctive Steve Ditko gestures so well suited for spell-casting—or web-shooting. A grim, atmospheric three-panel sequence follows, introducing us to a man tortured by nightmares—or rather, as we'll soon learn, by Nightmare, personified ruler of the Dimension of Dreams. Ditko plays up the rain dripping down the outside windows and ends on a campfire-style upshot on the man's face, eyes wide with fear and anguish, illuminated by the cigarette he's just lit with a match.

"I've heard a name," the man says, "spoken in whispers—Dr. Strange! He dabbles in black magic! Perhaps he can help me!"

Hard cut to that "side street" in Greenwich Village—identified in future stories as Bleecker Street, which is more of a main drag; but never mind that now. An Asian man, not yet named, answers the door and ushers our also-unnamed character into the presence of Doctor Strange, who promises to help him "by entering your dream!!!" (The three exclamation points show he means business.)

The story wastes no time on origins, preferring to show off Strange's power on the fly. This was a rarity at Marvel—*Spider-Man*, *The Fantastic Four*, and *The Hulk* all started off by chronicling the title heroes gaining their special abilities. It wasn't unusual for Ditko, though, as a survey of his later work shows. More important: Here it just *works*, stimulating the reader's curiosity as the panels fly by. Who is this guy? How did he get to this bizarre station in life? And who is "the Master, from whom all [his] powers stem"?

Ditko sticks to a nine-panel grid—three horizontal tiers of three panels each—one of the most traditional and economical of classic comic layouts. Twice he stretches that layout, cramming *four* panels into a tier: once for a ghostly flight across the world, and once to emphasize the hypnotic power of the character's mystic amulet. The art seems a little crowded, as you'd expect in such a short piece. But the storytelling is wonderful, as seen in two striking panels on page 2. First Ditko draws the magician's hand pointing upward in an "Aha" gesture, emphasizing the bizarre stipple-dotted texture on his glove. The very next shot places Strange in the foreground, while his visitor reacts in shock—as seen in the ornate mirror *behind* the main figure. An unusual bit of visual trickery for the time, and one that foreshadows Strange's trip "through the looking glass" to the realm of dreams, on the very next page.

But first, the sorcerer must prepare by sending his ghostly astral form to visit his aged mentor, the Ancient One. (Lee and Ditko didn't have all the series' nomenclature down yet—the Ancient One is called only "The Master" in this first story, and Strange's astral form is a "metaphysical spirit"; in the following issue it's his "spirit form.") In his very first appearance, the Ancient One tells Strange that "my days are numbered, and it is you who will some day take my place." That prediction will hang over the doctor's head for a decade to come; remember it as we make our way forward to 1973.

Then, with a reminder to use his amulet, the Ancient One sends Strange on his way. This entire sequence has taken up barely two-thirds of a page.

And we're on to Nightmare's Dream Dimension. Again, the skimpy page count limits what Ditko can show us; it's as if Salvador Dalí decided to paint a row of murals on postage stamps. Five months later, issue #116's "Return to the Nightmare World" will expand on this vision, allowing loose cross-hatchings to grow into stone walls, skeletal trees, and vast cobwebs whose dripping shapes suggest cruel smiles, glowing eyes. All of which, in turn, plants the seeds of the more expansive, elegantly drawn Dark Dimension of Dormammu.

But that's still to come, a bit more than a year into the series' future. Here and now, in the dreamworld, Strange meets a chained Jacob Marley figure with a pivotal plot clue on his withered lips—and then it's straight to Nightmare himself. When Strange calls Nightmare "my ancient foe," we feel as if we've been dropped into a fully realized world, with characters whose histories and pasts extend beyond the attic pages of *Strange Tales*. This, too, evokes the sensation of moving to a city, of striding down crowded sidewalks while thousands of personal dramas play out all around.

And *then*—as if the preceding 3.333 pages haven't covered enough ground!—Lee and Ditko feed us a twist. Out in the real world, the still-unnamed client who hired Strange realizes the magician has learned too much about the man's sins—which, we now learn, brought the whole dream-torment down on him in the first place. He decides to murder Strange by shooting the sorcerer's helpless, unmoving physical body. In the Dream Dimension, Nightmare taunts Strange with his impending death. So Strange reaches out mystically to the Ancient One, who activates the amulet worn by Strange's physical body (still with me?) and paralyzes the attacker.

Back home, Strange disarms the man and commands him to speak the truth. The would-be gunman agrees to confess his crimes, and Strange concludes: "It will be the only way you can ever sleep again."

It's remarkable how fully formed this series is, right from the start. Ditko and Lee introduce the hero, his powers, his mentor, the burden he bears, and the type of villain he'll go on to face on a regular basis—all while setting a distinct mood in a baroque, surreal milieu. Decades after its first publication, "Master of Black Magic!" still stands as one of the most gripping, efficient "pilot episodes" in comics history.

Only two main elements remained to be presented. Well, three, if you count Clea. But she's part of the series' next phase, a bit further on.

The first missing element is the doctor's house, his Sanctum Sanctorum. Oh, the house clearly exists in Ditko's mind. We're shown its ornate stone walls, its "ancient incense burner[s]," even the circular window whose distinctive glass pattern will become a hallmark of the series. That window recurs in issue #111, in the chambers of both Strange and the Ancient One, suggesting a mystic tradition related to the power they share. In issue #115, it's all over the Ancient One's secluded retreat.

But we don't actually see the house itself—its exterior, the place it exists on planet Earth—until issue #117. Until then it's a phantasm, a specter of the mind. An address handed to you on a worn slip of paper, with handwritten directions just vague enough to send you wandering the Village street-maze for an hour or two.

Cities were once like that: dangerous terrain filled with unspeakably glorious treasures. Looking to make a custom guitar? There's a place that sells exquisite inlaid rosettes, a storefront crouched among the gutted tenements and burned-out cars of Alphabet City. Want a bolt of beautiful cloth? Visit the garment district, where they list dangerously by the thousands under sky-high ceilings, the stock list kept only in the mind of the hunched-over proprietor. (Ask him "How much?" and he'll light a match, *setting the edge of the cloth on fire* to test its cotton count.)

In this age of computerized inventory and rapid home delivery—not to mention runaway gentrification—places like that are hard to conceive of, let alone remember. But if they existed, and they *did*, then how hard could it be to believe in a magical house, somewhere in that tangle of side streets, inhabited by a sorcerer with knowledge of realms beyond our own?

Not so hard. Not so strange. No stranger than finding a gem of a series sprouting in the back pages of an aging anthology comic, a magazine otherwise filled with *Fantastic Four* spinoffs and reprints of 1950s text stories.

The other missing piece of the Doctor Strange saga, after a grand total of five four-color pages, was a master villain. Nightmare had an air of eternal mystery to him, but his concerns only intersected with Doctor Strange's in a specific context (dreams). The series required a more human, personal touch; a villain linked deeply and inextricably to the hero himself.

"Face-to-Face with the Magic of Baron Mordo," in *Strange Tales* #111, filled that void. When the newly introduced Mordo launches an astral attack on Strange's mentor, we learn that he too trained with the Ancient One before choosing a darker, more selfish path. This fixes Strange firmly in the role of "good son" to the Ancient One, with Mordo as his opposite number.

All the basic tropes of the series are on display in these first two stories: astral projection, rapid interdimensional travel, the wisdom of the Ancient One, and the use of the amulet as a weapon in battle, fueled by its user's will power. Issue #111 ends on an ominous note as Strange says of Mordo: "I feel that death waits for one of us—the one who loses the next encounter!"

It didn't quite work out that way; either Lee or Ditko, or both, changed their minds in the three months before Doctor Strange reappeared in issue #114. Here's Stan's introductory blurb for that story:

In *Strange Tales* #110 and #111 we introduced the mystifying DR. STRANGE! Then we waited to receive your letters, to see if you would want him continued! Well, your enthusiastic mail left us only one choice, and so … we proudly present the third in our newest series …

"Mystifying" is a telling choice of words here. It's obviously meant to allude to the *mystic* powers of the character, but the word's actual meaning implies that the readers—and maybe even Stan himself—weren't yet quite sure what to make of this whole, umm, scene, baby.

The story begins with a sequence echoing the first tale: A "guest star" calls on Doctor Strange for help with a mystical problem. But we see, very quickly, that "Sir Clive Bentley" is actually Baron Mordo in disguise. We're still on a strict nine-panel grid here; aside from the larger splash-page image, the only time Ditko breaks the pattern is for a climactic astral plane clash between Strange and Mordo. And even that only takes up two of the nine "squares" in the grid.

We also meet Bentley's niece, Victoria, who's shown to have a "dormant talent for sorcery." This seems to imply a future for her in the strip; she does return eventually, but no one ever seemed to know quite what to do with her. (See Chapter 3.) Still, there's something appealing about Victoria, maybe because—despite her role as this issue's woman-in-jep—she comes off as a genuine adult. On the last page, she asks to become Strange's disciple, but he refuses in order to protect her from Mordo (who, contrary to the previous story's prediction, has survived the battle). "The more you learn," Strange warns her, "the more Baron Mordo will seek your life!"

In issue #115, we finally learn the origin of Stephen Strange. The flashback sequence paints a grim portrait of a brilliant, arrogant surgeon, brought low by an automobile accident that permanently damages the nerves in his hands. He becomes a "human derelict," prowling the docks of New York, until he hears of the Ancient One, whose magical powers may be able to restore his surgical ability.

Strange travels across the world to the Ancient One's mountain retreat—later stories place it in the Himalayas, but here it's only described as being in India. Strange regards the Ancient One's pupil—Mordo—as "creepy-looking," and scoffs at all the "meaningless scrolls" and "empty dirges." But when he learns that Mordo plans to kill the Ancient One, Strange stays on to protect his new master, thereby passing the first test of many to come.

Rereading this story today, it's the images of Strange on the docks, stringy hair blowing across his unshaven face, that really resonate. What if he hadn't found his redemption? You can almost picture him there today, bitter and restless, shivering in the pitiless wind. An old man, still searching for the magic.

The feature expands to eight pages with this issue—still barely enough to accommodate the origin. One notable detail: On page 5, the young Mordo prays to "Dormammu" for power. A small reference, soon to pay off in a big way.

The stories in issues #116–125 can best be described as transitional.

> THE ANCIENT ONE *!!* MANY TIMES IN THE PAST I, TOO, HAVE HEARD THIS NAME MENTIONED IN LOW WHISPERS *!* CAN IT BE THAT THERE IS SOME *TRUTH* TO THE LEGENDS ? HISTORY TELLS US THERE *HAVE* BEEN MEN WITH CERTAIN POWERS ... WHAT IF *HE* IS SUCH A MAN ?

Strange's power continues to grow; in #116, we see him cast an elaborate spell for the first time, and in #117 the Ancient One presents him with a mystic ring in addition to the ever-present amulet. In #120 the amulet rises up, for the first time, to form a third eye on his forehead, a Hindu- and Buddhist-inspired image that will recur much later. The stories increase in length again, first to nine pages and then to an even ten.

Ditko's trippy other-realm voyages alternate, here, with stories that show more of Stan's influence, such as the wax museum mystery of #121 and the Thor guest-shot in #123. "The Possessed," in issue #118, takes Strange to yet another hostile alt-dimension, but the story feels more like a stock sci-fi tale of alien invasion. It does, however, feature an unusually poetic boast from the doctor: "There is no power greater than that which I possess … for mine is the basic power of the imagination … the gossamer thread of which dreams are woven."

"Beyond the Purple Veil," in issue #119, shows the tension between the strip's mundane and surreal elements. The story opens with a pair of chatty burglars breaking into Strange's house, in a scene very reminiscent of the Lee-Ditko *Spider-Man* series. But the burglars are basically forgotten after Strange follows their trail to the Purple Dimension, where he battles its brutish, slave-holding ruler. When Strange returns home, the two men's fate is dismissed, off-panel, by a conveniently placed police officer.

While Lee and Ditko were crafting these tales, the Village was booming. "Unlicensed" coffee shops like the Four Winds and Café Elysee hosted readings of Beat poetry by Allan Ginsberg and Gregory Corso, filling the streets with folk music by the likes of Phil Ochs, Joni Mitchell, and the ever-present Bob Dylan. Sunday concert jams in Washington Square Park attracted crowds of young men in berets and work boots, women in flower-print dresses. New waves of culture, hot and thick, began to sweep the world forward on an irresistible tide.

Then, at the 1965 Newport Folk Festival, Dylan kicked things up a notch. To the shock of his fans, he performed with an electric guitar, amplifier, and backup band. He was still Bob Dylan, poet of the folk world; but now the sound was louder, the music tougher for the mainstream to ignore. It was time, he knew, to change up his game.

Strange Tales #126, just a few months earlier, marked a similar shift for Doctor Strange.

2

1964–1966: A Nameless Land, a Timeless Time

Ever since the launch of *Fantastic Four*, Stan Lee had crafted a character for himself, a carefully constructed editorial presence. He didn't just churn out press releases or standard house ads; he reminded the reader, repeatedly and with a cheeky dose of self-deprecation, just how awesome this entire enterprise was. How lucky they were to be living at this special time, to be a part of his Merry Marvel Marching Society.

Stan's over-the-top boasts ("A TALE DESTINED TO BECOME A MAGNIFICENT MILESTONE IN THE MARVEL AGE OF COMICS!") owed a debt to circus ringleaders, carnival barkers, and Borscht Belt comedians—professions that were already slipping into history by the early 1960s. But somehow, the combination caught the eye of the rising youth culture. Part of it was the winking, ironic voice; another part was surely the larger-than-life images of Jack Kirby and the otherworldly quirkiness of Steve Ditko's work. Stan also welcomed interaction with readers in letter columns, fanzines, conventions, and, later, on college campuses.

Ditko, by contrast, had no use for what the fanzines called "egoboo" (ego-boosting). He attended exactly one comic book convention, in 1964, then retreated from direct contact with his fans. Over the decades, he developed a reputation as a loner— even as he maintained a Manhattan studio where he continued to draw his own, idiosyncratic comics.

In an odd way, cities are made for people like that. One of the draws of a New York, a Paris, or a Copenhagen is that you can live in solitude while surrounded by people. For a certain type of artistic temperament, that lifestyle holds a strong appeal.

In 1964, Ditko requested, and was granted, full control over plotting the Doctor Strange feature. He also took back the inking duties, which had been farmed out for the past few months to veteran artist George Roussos (credited as George Bell). At the time, comics were usually produced on an assembly-line basis, with one artist drawing the book in pencil and another rendering it in crisp, reproducible India ink. Some artists, including Ditko, preferred to control both steps in the process.

"The Domain of the Dread Dormammu" explodes out of *Strange Tales* #126 with the blinding light of a mystic amulet. The opening page plunges the reader into the chaotic Dark Dimension; the figure of Doctor Strange, pointedly small in the swirling chaos, might be conjuring a spell or just flailing helplessly for his life. The story wastes no time in transporting Strange to this world of magic-carpet platforms, multi-armed stone cyclopes, and Cubist doorways opening wide to spiral paths in the air. All ruled by Dormammu, a tyrant whose very face is flame, who sits on his air-throne surrounded by archways and sycophants and floating, ectoplasmic viewscreens.

Suddenly the whole series just seems to *move*. It's as if Ditko and Lee picked up their electric guitars, strummed the loudest chord they could imagine, and let the wall of sound propel them into the future.

On the last page, Strange comes face to face with Dormammu. And the ground drops out beneath our feet as we realize we're reading the first continued story in the series' history.

I haven't even mentioned Clea—or, as she's known in these first appearances, "the mystery girl in the diabolical dimension." Pale and striking in sworl-patterned tights and wide pink collars, her blue-and-ivory hair styled into bizarre leonine shapes, she shadows Strange at a distance as he fights his way past Dormammu's defenses. Clea's presence is another first for the strip: She's a potential love interest, yes, but as a native of the Dark Dimension, she also serves as a sort of narrator, a single-voiced Greek chorus explaining this topsy-turvy realm to Strange (and to us). His goal, to remove the threat of Dormammu, doesn't wind up being as clear-cut as he expects; but even if he succeeds, he clearly won't do it without Clea's help.

As with Nightmare—who, again, sometimes felt like a rehearsal for Dormammu—the ruler of the Dark Dimension has a past with the Ancient One. That struggle stretches back decades, perhaps eons. The title of #127, "Duel with the Dread Dormammu," leads the reader to expect a fairly stock hero-villain battle. But Ditko and Lee throw a wrench into the other-dimensional works when Clea explains the threat of the Mindless Ones—brutish cyclopean monsters held at bay from the Dark Dimension only by Dormammu's mystic shield.

"You must not defeat him," Clea says of Dormammu. "Only he can save us from the Mindless Ones!"

"Yet, if he lives," Strange replies, grimacing, "humanity shall always be in danger."

Zack Kruse, in his fascinating book *Mysterious Travelers: Steve Ditko and the Search for a New Liberal Identity*, analyzes this conflict in terms of Ditko's evolving, largely Objectivist political views. To Kruse, Dormammu represents tyranny, with the Mindless Ones standing in for mob rule. Which is preferable? Or maybe, more to the point: Which is the lesser evil?

In the end Strange compromises, agreeing to halt the duel in order to help Dormammu against the Mindless Ones. The Dark Dimension is sketchily portrayed in this story; even in twenty pages, the creators could only cover so much ground, and Ditko's focus is clearly on the surreal, Dalí-esque landscape.

But we're led to believe it's inhabited by a sizable population of ordinary people, a sort of Soviet Russia riddled with dimensional portals and ribboned skywalks. Strange cannot ignore those innocents, the bystanders caught between his power and that of his enemy.

Together, they force back the Mindless Ones. This enrages Dormammu: "Curse you, mortal! Curse the fact that I needed your help! Curse the woeful fate that has placed me in your debt!" Strange, realizing Dormammu "has his own moral code," agrees to leave. He demands only two things: Clea must not be harmed, and Dormammu must "vow never to invade the Earth."

I'll admit I'm wincing as I transcribe some of this dialogue. For one thing—and this is in no way a failing of the original work—it was meant to be hand-lettered in all caps, sandwiched between volleys of force-beams, not set in cold type and read as part of a continuous stream of prose. But the stories are also a product of their time. As I write this, sixty-plus years have passed since Stan got these pages in the office, held them up to the light to figure out what Ditko was up to, and applied his trademark light touch to the dialogue. That's a long time, more than three times the interval between World War II and 1964.

Yet another factor: Whatever their literary and artistic ambitions, Lee and Ditko knew their primary audience was children. College-age readers were already discovering

Marvel—patrons of Café Reggio and the Village Gate discussed the Ancient One over cappuccino and cheap beer, right alongside their analyses of Andy Warhol and James Baldwin. But the publishers still needed a few years to catch up.

Whatever the reasons, Stan's patter—written at speed with the clear goal of keeping the stories grounded—disguises the fact that there's some pretty serious philosophizing going on in the Dark Dimension. In the later Steve Englehart/Frank Brunner stories, which I encountered *first*, the dialogue is similarly grandiose but the philosophy is spelled out more overtly—often in the musings and monologues of Doctor Strange himself. (One feature that stays consistent throughout this ten-year period: Even for a Marvel character, Strange talks to himself a *lot*.)

As a kid, I found some of the Lee/Ditko material overblown and distancing. As an adult, I can appreciate the fact that, paradoxically, this actually makes the philosophy *subtler* than in the later stories.

At the end of issue #127, the Ancient One rewards Doctor Strange with "a new cape, and a more wondrous amulet." The amulet seems pretty much the same, but the distinctive red cape becomes the last piece of the character's distinctive costume— which remains intact, with minor alterations, to this day. In issue #128, we learn that the cape allows him to fly; in later appearances, it's known as the Cloak of Levitation. The Ancient

One also repeats his prediction from issue #110: One day, he will pass on and Doctor Strange will inherit both his power and his weighty, almost unimaginable responsibilities.

Lee and Ditko follow the Dark Dimension story with a more grounded, Earthbound tale. In *Strange Tales* #128, a villain called only "the Demon" hatches his schemes from "a locked sub-cellar deep within the canyons of the great city." But this proves to be a brief change-up. Issue #129's "Tiboro! Tyrant of the Sixth Dimension!" begins with a group of scientists dismissing magic as "fiction" and proclaiming that "Dr. Strange's theories are as ridiculous as his attire." (Ouch.) Strange refuses to appear on TV with the scientists and, when they finally admit to the existence of magic, wipes the knowledge from their minds in order to keep his own secrets. That decision feels much more like the publicity-shy Ditko than the publicly boisterous Lee, who did not script this issue—it's a rare fill-in by Marvel veteran Don Rico.

Strange Tales #130 marks another milestone, in a few different ways. It's the first time Doctor Strange is featured on the cover, an event Stan brags about in the blurb itself. Baron Mordo's sneak-attack on Strange makes for a powerful cover image, but it's not by Ditko; Jack Kirby does the honors. The right two-fifths of the cover are taken up with another blurb showing the Human Torch and the Thing in Beatle wigs! Truly, with this issue, the 1960s have stormed ashore at Marvel.

More importantly, this issue begins a seventeen-part serial that will conclude with the end of Steve Ditko's tenure on Doctor Strange. Briefly: Dormammu, having vowed not to attack the Earth, gets around the letter of his agreement by powering up Mordo to do it instead. This shows the depth of Ditko's planning; once again, Mordo was seen appealing to Dormammu for power as far back as issue #115.

When Mordo's assault drives Strange out of his home, we begin to learn about a community of mystics scattered around the world, many of them with motives and grievances of their own. Even the Ancient One's financial advisor(!) makes an appearance, briefly providing sanctuary to the hunted sorcerer. Issue #131 continues the story with Strange, in disguise, luring Mordo to an airport while he hides in a crate.

It plays like a spy story, and considering that it's new territory for the series, it all works stunningly well. Ditko seems to relish rendering the shadowy streets and waterfront of Hong Kong, alternating with the surreal portals of the Dark Dimension. In #132, the stakes rise again as the feverish Ancient One mutters, "If only Strange could know of— Eternity!", the first mention of that crucial name. Then, just as Mordo is about to fall to Strange in combat, Dormammu takes full possession of him and blasts Strange into some unknown realm.

Ditko and Lee continue to play minor chords echoing the major themes of the series. In #133, Strange—having fled blind across the realms—helps defeat an evil sorceress, a sort of dark mirror of himself: She learned the mystic arts from a master, then murdered him. By #135, "Eternity Beckons," Strange recognizes Dormammu as his true foe. Levels of power begin to come clear: Mordo doesn't know the meaning of Eternity, but Dormammu does, and declares that Strange must not be allowed to find it/him/them.

Strange spends most of #137 inside the mind of the weakened Ancient One, searching for the secret of Eternity—this sets up the climax of the 1973 Shuma-Gorath storyline, which we'll cover in Chapter 5. Clea returns, sporting a stylish new pink turtleneck—clearly the latest, "gearest" craze in the Dark Dimension. In #138, the series levels up once again. Ditko pours his all into the "dazzling, description-defying dimension of … Eternity" (that's our Stan!), depicting an expansive, angular dream space crammed with crystal pathways, wide platforms and portals, an atomic microverse ("a world within a world!"), and shimmering cosmic backdrops.

As Strange watches, the microverse begins to shift and grow—and, in a rare full-page interior panel, transforms into a huge cloaked figure comprising stars/planets/galaxies inside its ethereal body. With a single gesture, Eternity learns all of Strange's secrets, and then—to the sorcerer's shock—denies him the help he seeks against Mordo and Dormammu. "You already possess the means to defeat your foes," Eternity declares. "Events have occurred which require a key … and *wisdom* is that key."

Before Strange can decode that little mystic riddle, he returns home to find that Mordo has captured the Ancient One. In #139, Mordo and Strange mix it up again. When Mordo botches the job—again—Dormammu steps in personally, transporting the combatants, including the Ancient One, to "a distant, neutral dimension" (#140). Dormammu invites the rulers of neighboring realms to attend the battle, leading the Ancient One to exclaim: "Alien despots whose names are spoken in whispers!"

This expands the scope of the series once again as we see the fear Dormammu inspires, even among these otherwise powerful tyrants. They don't seem to like him very much, but they're happy enough to back him, possibly because they, too, all seem to want to invade the Earth. (Why? It's not explained. Back then, everyone wanted to invade the Earth.)

By all accounts, Ditko and Lee were working separately by this time, their lines of communication strained if not severed. You'd never know it, though, as the story continues to barrel onward, sure-handed as ever. Dormammu challenges Strange to a rematch—but not with spells, force bolts, or amulets.

"Our only weapons shall be our mystic minds … and these enchanted Pincers of Power!"

And what, exactly, are the Pincers of Power? Why, they're wrist-mounted disks that project ectoplasmic, sort of, pliers(?) that can grab or shoot energy through the user's opponent. A weapon so important that a pivotal chapter of the saga is named after it, yet cartoonishly simple in its design. In that way, the Pincers embody the basic dichotomy of Doctor Strange: the cosmic and the mundane.

Ditko varies the action nicely as Strange struggles to master the Pincers, finally wielding them with sufficient skill to defeat the more experienced Dormammu. ("Wisdom is the key.") In #141, a furious Dormammu swears not to invade Earth—again—but in his fury, he banishes both Clea and Mordo to distant realms. The story ends with three ticking bombs, one of them literal: Dormammu taunts Strange with the fate of Clea, the Ancient One tasks him with stopping "traces of evil enchantment that Mordo has spread all over Earth," and Mordo's former agents plant an actual, physical time bomb inside the Sanctum Sanctorum.

As we return to Earth in #142, Lee and Ditko continue to flesh out an entire world of magic-users, all plotting against each other in secret. Three of these sorcerers capture Strange, encasing him in a creepy metal mask that covers his face, with blocky restraints on his hands. (At the time, Ditko was sharing a studio with noted mid-century fetish artist Eric Stanton, and may have ghosted some work for him.) "My cloak of levitation is gone," Strange laments. "My enchanted amulet has been taken from me! My physical body is still helpless—only my weaker spirit form is able to move—to see—!"

And with his hero reduced to this low point, Stan Lee abruptly exits the series. He stays on as editor—there's nobody else in the office!—but he turns over the scripting, in succession, to a pair of new writers.

With issue #143, a young Roy Thomas briefly assumes that role. Thomas, then Lee's assistant, later became editor-in-chief of the company during a period of great expansion. He's also a prolific writer who shaped the course of Marvel into the 1970s and beyond—including a crucial run on *Doctor Strange* that we'll cover in Chapter 3. Here, however, it's still Ditko's show. The story's title, "With None Beside Me," could refer to the artist's solitary plotting methods as well as (obviously) the perils of the masked and manacled Doctor Strange.

In #144, we revisit the rulers of other dimensions, with their tangle of concerns and allegiances. The series is clearly wending its way back to the Dark Dimension for a third go-round. In the final panel, Strange thinks, "I must soon return to rescue her who once helped me!" (That's Clea, still unnamed.) "Then, Dormammu and I may find ourselves in final mortal combat."

The next two stories feature dialogue by Dennis (Denny) O'Neil, a well-loved writer whose work would soon help revolutionize several of DC's older characters. Like Thomas, he joins Doctor Strange very early in his writing career—in his case, as we'll see, at an even more difficult juncture. Issue #145 features one of the now-familiar "Doctor Strange prepares himself on Earth" interludes, notable for a scene where an attacker shoots our hero with an ordinary pistol.

And then there's the climactic issue #146. In this ten-page finale, Dormammu faces off against Eternity, with Strange and Clea caught in the middle.

Fans still remember the two full-page shots depicting the climactic clash—"Human eyes have never witnessed such a struggle!" O'Neil's Strange thinks. And yet, it's hard to escape the feeling that we're rushing toward a finale. Eternity, a fascinating concept, vanishes almost before we've gotten to know him. Even the Ancient One, as he rescues Strange, says, "Dormammu is no more … I know not the fate of Eternity."

But the story's final sequence carries a different, quiet sort of power. Clea finally tells Strange her name—a touching moment, after all they've done for each other. Their duties still lie in different worlds, but as she waves farewell, Strange says, "I feel in my heart that it is our destiny to meet again."

And with that, Ditko too is gone.

His reasons remain his own. In a 2015 essay, he cites Stan's refusal to deal directly with him anymore as a deciding factor—but that account doesn't fully explain the background of the dispute, and in any case it focuses primarily on *Spider-Man*. A longstanding rumor holds that Ditko had actually penciled two additional Doctor Strange stories. Artist Russ Maheras reported that Ditko, years later, confirmed this rumor in his studio and pointed to a pile of art. But Ditko refused to let his visitor see the pages.

It's almost irresistible to speculate on what Ditko had planned. The Dormammu/Eternity clash could easily have been expanded, allowing for further exploration of the villain's plans, the meaning of Eternity, and Clea's place in the drama. But that's just conjecture. With Ditko's passing, we'll never know.

Strange Tales #146 bears a cover date of July 1966; the Grand Comics Database logs it as hitting newsstands in April. That same month, Bob Dylan embarked on an extensive tour of Europe and Australia, performing a set split sharply in half. The first half of the show featured the singer performing solo with his trademark harmonica and acoustic guitar. In the second half, a full electric band backed him up, playing the songs that had drawn boos at the Folk Festival a year before. The times were a-changing, but they hadn't changed all the way yet.

Doctor Strange was about to enter his own period of creative transition. The character had begun to gather a following in the counterculture, appearing notably in *The Electric Kool-Aid Acid Test*, author Tom Wolfe's journalistic profile of the pro-drug Merry Pranksters. (Wolfe cited Doctor Strange as an obsession of the Pranksters' leader, novelist/Beat icon Ken Kesey.) But except for covers and guest appearances, no one other than Steve Ditko had ever drawn Doctor Strange. Could Marvel keep the magic alive?

3

1966–1969: Other Realms, Other Voices

Whatever the circumstances of Steve Ditko's departure, one thing is sure: He gave virtually no notice. With *Strange Tales* on a strict monthly schedule, Editor Stan had to shift gears fast, scrambling to produce a story for the next issue. Writer Stan stepped back in to lend a hand—for five pages, anyway.

Issue #147's "From the Nameless Nowhere Comes … Kaluu!" shows the strain. For one thing, despite his title-card billing, Kaluu isn't even mentioned until page 9; only his eyes make an actual appearance, in the very last panel of the story. Doctor Strange spends several pages reviewing his recent exploits in the Dark Dimension, a device that turns the proceedings into a sort of "clip show" padded out with reprinted Ditko panels.

Dr. STRANGE MASTER OF THE MYSTIC ARTS!

"FROM THE NAMELESS NOWHERE COMES...
KALUU!

EVEN IN NEW YORK'S FAMOUS, FANTASTIC, FAR-OUT **GREENWICH VILLAGE**, WHERE EVERY OTHER PASSERBY IS A COLORFUL, KOOKIE CHARACTER, THE DRAMATIC FIGURE OF **DR. STRANGE** STILL RECEIVES ITS SHARE OF STARTLED GLANCES ON THOSE RARE OCCASIONS WHEN THE MYSTERIOUS MASTER OF THE MYSTIC ARTS VENTURES FORTH, IN FULL VIEW OF THE CITY'S TEEMING POPULACE! SO IT IS ON THIS FATEFUL NIGHT OF NIGHTS ---

SINCE MY LENGTHY BATTLE WITH THE DREAD **DORMAMMU**, THIS HAS BEEN MY FIRST OPPORTUNITY TO EMBARK UPON A RELAXING TOUR OF EVERYDAY **SHOPPING**!

HOW **GOOD** IT IS TO MINGLE ONCE MORE WITH MY FELLOW MEN --TO SHARE THE PROSAIC DAILY ROUTINE OF THE CITY DWELLER!

ZOWIE! HE'S THE EVER-LOVIN' **GEAREST!** FAR AS I'M CONCERNED, THE MODS HAVE **HAD** IT! THAT CRAZY CAPE REALLY COMES ON **STRONG!**

THE START OF A WONDROUS NEW JOURNEY INTO THE SHADOWY WORLD OF THE SUPER-NATURAL!

MAN! LIKE **THERE'S A BOSS** BUNCH'A THREADS! THAT DAD IS GOTTA BE WHAT'S **HAPPENIN'!**

SCRIPT: (PGS. 1-5) STAN LEE.. (OUR VACATIONIN' SORCERER)
SCRIPT: (PGS. 6-10) DENNY O'NEIL-- (OUR SORCERER'S APPRENTICE)
ART: BILLY EVERETT... (OUR PEERLESS PRESTIDIGITATOR)
LETTERING: SAM ROSEN.. (OUR NAIVE NECROMANCER)
AMULET POLISHER: IRV FORBUSH.. (OUR STOWAWAY)

TWO'LL GET YA TEN THAT GUY'S **DOC STRANGE** HIMSELF! HE'S THE JOKER WHO'S ALWAYS PUTTIN' EVERYONE **ON** WITH ALL THAT HOCUS-POCUS JAZZ!

The rest of the art is by Bill Everett, a brilliant writer-artist best known as the creator of Marvel's Sub-Mariner, a wartime character he returned to several times during his career. Over the years, Stan had used Everett as a "fixer" on troubled series like *Venus*, a bizarre 1950s hybrid of office romance and Greco-Roman mythology that switched genres every few issues. Everett's work on Strange, what little there is in this first story, shows off his gifts for character, street detail, and cinematic camera angles. It's also a pretty sharp swerve from Ditko's simpler, more stylized imagery.

Page 1 shows a change of priorities right from the start—probably Stan's, maybe with contributions from Everett. Doctor Strange strides down a city street so detailed, so packed with people that it almost resembles a photograph, a still from some *verité* film of the period. A thick-bodied man with a cane, a young woman in sunglasses and miniskirt, a straight-arrow businessman wearing Clark Kent's hat—they fill the page, showing us that this, this very real neighborhood, is where Stephen Strange lives.

In case all that's too subtle, Stan lays down a machine-gun spray of hipster/Beat thought balloons, showing us exactly how this array of "colorful, kookie character[s]" regard their mystically inclined neighbor. A young woman turns to Strange, thinking, "Zowie! He's the ever-lovin' gearest!" A turtlenecked character frowns under his beret, grumbling about Strange's "hocus-pocus jazz." A bearded Beatnik observes, with more enthusiasm than grammar: "Now there's a boss bunch'a threads! That dad is gotta be what's happenin'!"

With a primary creative force—Ditko—removed from the picture, it made sense to play to the new artist's strengths. But this page also shows, quite forcefully, how Stan Lee saw Doctor Strange: the coolest guy in the Village. A hybrid of respected authority figure and with-it writer/performer; a local luminary, a figure his neighbors know and recognize when he pops down the street to the apothecary. Above all, a *relatable* figure, fitting neatly into the then-evolving culture of celebrity. The Allen Ginsberg, the Dylan, the Phil Ochs—maybe even the *Stan Lee*—of magic.

Other worlds, trippy dimensions are fine—an undeniable source of the character's appeal. But the street is where it's at.

So Lee and Everett kick off the story by demonstrating the character's ambivalence toward fame, then send him jumping through a series of distinctly non-mystical hoops. In quick succession, Strange places an order with his druggist; stops a street mugging; discusses money problems with his servant, Wong; and deals with a visit from city inspectors, who demand he upgrade his home to comply with building codes.

We haven't dealt with Wong yet, have we? Soon. Soon.

Then, either because of deadlines or the press of his other

duties, Stan turns the back half of the story over to Denny O'Neil. Following the Dark Dimension slide show, the Ancient One drops in for a couple of pages to warn us about dear old Kaluu. The "next issue" caption—almost certainly added by Stan—promises "a story so bizarre you may never be able to forget it … the origin of the Ancient One!"

As Stan *also* used to say: Marvel marches on.

I haven't mentioned it yet, but by this time Doctor Strange shared the pages of *Strange Tales* with Nick Fury, Agent of S.H.I.E.L.D.—a postwar espionage series originally helmed by Lee and Jack Kirby, and soon to be revolutionized by pop-art writer-artist Jim Steranko. With only one exception, Fury headlined the book, dominating the covers. Strange was represented only by a small inset panel or, sometimes, just a blurb …

… until Ditko's departure from Doctor Strange. From that point on—and yes, it's odd timing, but probably a coincidence—there's a gradual but steady increase in the feature's prominence. With issue #146, Ditko's last, the two series begin alternating as sole cover feature. On #150, a simple proto-logo reading DOCTOR STRANGE crowds in next to Fury's. With #156 the order is reversed, so Strange's logo comes first; from then on they alternate positions, so the featured character's logo reads first above its corresponding illustration. As of #164 the main logo becomes much larger, with a small "and Nick Fury, Agent of S.H.I.E.L.D.," or "and Doctor Strange," in plain hand-lettering below.

Two possibilities here, which aren't mutually exclusive. Either Nick Fury was slipping as a sales draw, leading Marvel to try giving Doctor Strange more play; or, especially toward the end, the impending launch of separate titles starring both features encouraged the publisher to give them equal prominence. But we'll get to that.

For now we've got artist Bill Everett and, as of issue #148, O'Neil on scripts. The Grand Comic Database lists issues #147–168 as a single 22-part story, and it is, sort of: a story that's plotted by many hands, changes direction on the fly, shifts tones and milieus almost at random, reverses itself from one installment to the next, and leaves plot holes hanging for months until the next writer remembers to plug them.

At the time, of course, neither Stan nor anyone else thought this material would be remembered, collected, or reread in sequence by anyone other than a handful of hardcore back-issue hunters. In the age before digital purchases—before, even, book-format collections!—comics occupied a unique, liminal space in the world of mass media. On the one hand, they weren't in any way a performance-based medium. The process of comics creation resembled a group of musicians going into the studio, not a band on tour.

But there the analogy breaks down. Other media would be released in "permanent" forms—records, tapes, books, and chapbooks. Records and books didn't always stay in print, but that was the goal. In contrast, there was nothing *permanent* about comics. After a story appeared once, its only chance for a reprint was in the back of an equally ephemeral annual or reprint comic. The pattern was almost cruel: You bought a comic book, you read it, and eventually someone threw it away. Even many fans viewed their hobby as a degraded, easily dismissed form of fiction.

All of which suggests an excuse—if not a rationale—for the scattershot, throw-talent-at-the-wall approach of Doctor Strange's next two years. Even if some publisher, someday, were to lose their mind and decide to collect Marvel comics in book form—why surely, in that barely conceivable scenario, they'd only be interested in the heavy hitters. Spider-Man, the Fantastic Four, maybe the Avengers. How could the comic publishers of the day envision a world where *everything* would be preserved? How would they have thought the back features in *Strange Tales* between 1966 and 1968 would ever be *seen* again?

That said, there's fun to be had in these issues—some trippy art from top-flight veterans, some young talents stretching their creative muscles. But the days of Steve Ditko's firm storytelling hand are definitely behind us. Bill Everett crafts a striking design for Kaluu, the new Big Bad, but the story glides over some resonant material: In his first battle with Kaluu, 500 years ago, the Ancient One apparently killed most of the villagers he was trying to save.

Roy Thomas pops back in to script a single issue—#150—whose cover blurb, "Exit Kaluu … Enter Umar!", sounds a wee bit frantic. This Kaluu guy, he's not working? Not formidable, not *gear* enough? Okay, thank you for coming. NEXT!

Regarding Umar: As the sister of Dormammu, she brings a welcome note of diversity to the Doctor Strange boys' club of tyrants and conquerors. (Her name is given as "Kara" in the previous issue's "next" blurb—more evidence of last-minute gear-shifting.) She returns to the Dark Dimension to reclaim her throne, following Dormammu's disappearance in the whole Eternity dust-up. This wraps up a loose end that both Marvel and Doctor Strange seemed to forget, in the wake of Ditko's departure: With Dormammu vanquished, there's nothing to stop the Mindless Ones from invading and overrunning the Dark Dimension.

In a few short panels, Umar banishes the Mindless Ones, "succeed[ing] where even the Dreaded One failed." This establishes her power, but it also sets up an odd situation: The two siblings don't actually appear together until much later.

With #151 Stan returns as scripter, and in #153, Marie Severin takes over as primary artist. Severin, a prolific and talented artist and colorist, brings a quirky, kinetic style to her first series for 1960s Marvel. She draws nice chunky monsters and a terrific Ancient One, but she, too, lasts less than a year on the series.

Two weeks later, as readers awaited "The Death of Clea," the Smog of 1966 descended over the city. New Yorkers endured a strictly-indoor Thanksgiving as particulate counts rose to crisis levels, coating roofs and windows in layers of toxic soot. Clea *didn't* die in the end, but dozens of others did—the city's daily fatality rate rose, temporarily, by double digits.

The smog had receded, if not vanished, by the time #156 promised "Next: The End of the Ancient One!" Those next-issue blurbs were causing no end of trouble, and as if to prove it, Doctor Strange's mentor meets a hasty, confusing death in the opening pages of #157. Fused with a pillar of stone, the Ancient One croaks out, "My power now is yours! Use it wisely …" then manages a few enigmatic warnings before gasping his last.

This moment was foretold, of course, in the very first Doctor Strange story (see Chapter 1). But fans expected a better, and better timed, passing of the torch from master to disciple. Much later, they'd get it.

The last page of this issue introduces the Living Tribunal, a pretty sharp character design on Severin's part. With #158 Roy Thomas joins the team again, and things get trippy as the Tribunal accuses Strange of upsetting some eternal balance of the realms. For the first time since Ditko, the strip begins to gather some forward motion, a sense of creative vision.

Unfortunately, the next ten issues continue the merry-go-round of writers. Raymond Marais scripts #160–161; he gets points for the flirty page-one blurb: "Well, we've got the book! So if you got the bell and candle—what are we waitin' for?" (That might have been Stan, but the innuendo doesn't *quite* sound like him.) In the same issue, latent mystic Victoria Bentley returns as a hypnotized thrall to Baron Mordo. She'll play a larger part in the series' next incarnation.

Jim Lawrence, a newspaper strip writer, takes over for five issues—his only Marvel work. Then it falls to Denny to bat cleanup in #167–168.

The steady creative hand during this period is artist Dan Adkins, who receives plotting credit in at least one issue. Adkins brings classic pulp stylings, great creatures and alien worlds, and a refreshingly open storytelling style to the proceedings. He's been credited with—and blamed for—moving the strip in an openly sci-fi direction, introducing Nebulon, Lord of the Planets Perilous, and the vicious robot Voltorg (also called Voltorr, sometimes—yes, spellcheck, I feel your pain).

But the primary villain is a self-styled "Scientist Supreme" called Yandroth—an obvious attempt to pit Strange against an enemy with skills diametrically opposed to his own. "The cold, relentless power of science versus the occult force of the magic arts," Strange muses. "Never have I dreamed of facing such a challenge!" For his part, Yandroth's dialogue sometimes resembles a bizarre mirror-image of Strange's, with exclamations like: "By the ninth theorem of anti-matter!"

It's a game try at a new approach, and the art remains stylish, but the whole thing still doesn't quite gel. In #166–167 the Ancient One returns, with a dizzyingly brief explanation of his survival. In #168 Strange rescues Victoria, banishes Yandroth to "fall endlessly through the Dimension of Dreams," and returns home—where a final blurb promises "Next: Doctor Strange in his own mag at last!"

Wait, what?

Strange Tales #168 hit newsstands in early 1968, a tumultuous year that saw America grapple with a wave of political assassinations, a contentious Presidential election, and the escalating carnage in Vietnam—brought into millions of living rooms, for the first time ever, on televised evening news broadcasts.

At Marvel, though, most of the news was positive. A greatly improved distribution arrangement allowed the company, for the first time in years, to ramp up the number of books it published. In one of its first moves, Marvel promoted both Nick Fury and Doctor Strange from the crowded barracks of *Strange Tales* into their own, separate titles.

Fury got his own issue #1, while Strange's numbering carried right on from *Strange Tales*. This wasn't a sign of disrespect. In those days, continuing the numbering allowed *Doctor Strange* to retain the former book's subscription mailing privileges, and might have made newsstand placement easier too. And so, four weeks after that final *Strange Tales*, *Doctor Strange* #169 became the first comic ever published with the character's name in its title.

Roy Thomas returns as writer, this time for good; he will write every non-reprint page of the next fifteen issues. Adkins stays on as artist, one of only two pencillers to handle the new book regularly. Doctor Strange could no longer hide in the back of an anthology title; readers had to be motivated to buy the book for him and him alone. That required a steady creative hand, an end to the constantly shifting lineup of writers and artists.

The stories had already begun to grow looser, with fewer panels per page—a trend that had started with Kirby and spread quickly throughout the Marvel line. It made plotting easier but it also played to Adkins's strengths, letting him spread out to show bizarre worlds and unearthly vistas. Now, with nearly twice as many pages in each story, the effect was doubled. Full- and double-page panels became common; action scenes often sprawled out over eight, ten, or more pages.

In #169, Thomas and Adkins retell the character's origin, a common trick in a new first issue. The flashback follows the original story closely, with only two added details. A doctor who asks the young, arrogant Strange to do charity work receives a name, Dr. Benton. The other change explains an element of the origin: After the accident that damages his hands, Strange spends all his money on medical procedures to restore his own surgical ability. The procedures fail, leading him to that fateful night as "an aimless drifter, a familiar sight on the fog-bound docks."

The flashback even keeps the beat-up cigarette in the unshaven Strange's lips. In fact, the issue's pages *reek* of nicotine. Pre-accident Strange enjoys a triumphant cig after a successful operation; one dockworker holds out a pack of smokes to the other as they discuss the Ancient One. In the present-day framing sequence Strange, plagued by insomnia, lights up a smoke that lasts him all the way to page 20. Not exactly a portrait of a surgeon healing himself, and *definitely* not something you'd see in a comic today. Maybe it was just cold in the Ancient One's Himalayan retreat.

In issue #171, Strange enlists Victoria Bentley's help to find the missing Clea. By bringing in Victoria as a potential romantic rival, Thomas introduces, for the first time in the strip, a touch of soap-opera melodrama—an element that had already become a hallmark of the Marvel line. When Strange and Clea are reunited in #172, we cut away to Victoria, crying to herself: "I always knew it would be this way … when he found the fair Clea for whom he sought! But still, could I ever have refused him … when he asked me to help find her? For, may Heaven forgive me … I *love him* …!"

This triangle continues, off and on, for several issues. The dialogue is obviously of its time, but both women are treated with considerable respect; Victoria suffers in silence, never telling Strange how she feels. To save his life, she teams up with Clea—whom she barely knows—without hesitating for a second. But there's never any doubt who has captured Strange's heart. "I see now that the one I love can never be mine," Victoria notes, in a weirdly deadpan moment, "for, what competition can one whose powers are merely latent, be for a girl from another universe?"

With #172, Gene Colan and Tom Palmer come on as the regular art team. It's lovely, stylish work, perfectly suited to the material. Colan's adventurous storytelling takes full advantage of the longer, twenty-page format; his portrayal of New York feels utterly real, just as it would a few years later in the cult-favorite series *Howard the Duck*. Palmer's lush, illustrative line firms up Colan's loose faces just enough to sharpen the expressions, and his use of zipatone adds an element of shadow to select scenes.

More than any previous artist, Colan also draws a very sexy Clea—and a pretty hot Stephen Strange, too. After her arrival on Earth, they strut through the streets like a hippie power couple, the Mick Jagger and Marianne Faithful of the mystical set. Their first stroll through the Village, in #174, attracts so much attention that Clea loses her temper and magics a truck into vapor. Celebrities!

Clea can be forgiven her little anxieties; she's worried by Strange's demeanor, mistaking his astral meditations for doubts about their relationship. This development suggests some potentially stormy, even controversial relationship dynamics, but it's pretty much dropped after one more ominous development: When Strange sets her up in a new apartment, Clea kisses him for the first time, in a moody, silent sequence. And what does he do? Runs straight off to England in response to a call from Victoria.

Even as that little red flag is being raised, Charity Doctor Benton from the revised origin drops in, demanding to see Doctor Strange. He tells Wong that Strange was once "a real doctor … a brilliant surgeon … not the gaudily dressed charlatan that he has since become!" Benton wants to hire Strange as a consultant—in essence, to convince the hippie to drop back *in* to society and get a real job. This whole plot is, well, kind of a drag, man, which is probably why Thomas shifts it into a different gear pretty fast.

Speaking of Wong, we're overdue for a quick digression on him. As the Asian servant to a privileged white man, his portrayal in these stories could be construed as offensive. Certainly it's a product of its time, following the template of an even earlier era of white-centric pulp stories. Lee and Ditko, for their part, used the character sparingly—and right from the strip's beginning, it's clear that Doctor Strange has his own master. We see this as late as 1972's *Marvel Premiere* #4, where

Strange apologizes to Wong for snapping at him, then defers to "the venerated Ancient One."

Wong's obsequiousness stands out more in this run of stories, largely because the character has more to do—his role expands along with the page count. But Thomas consistently portrays him as competent and professional. As time goes on, Wong's relationship with Strange will become closer to one of equals; but unfortunately, that's still quite a ways off.

Meanwhile, there's plenty of widescreen action going on. Umar and Dormammu play sibling power games in the Dark Dimension; Nekron, an Orson Welles-ish sorcerer, summons a mob called the Sons of Satannish, whose leader hypnotizes Clea and sends her off to kill our hero. With issue #177, some behind-the-scenes plot mechanics begin to show. The cover features a creepy-looking Strange in full, skintight facemask/hood; the blurb proclaims: "Hail the Master!" Again, wait. What?

Here's the in-story explanation: After exiling Strange and Clea to another dimension, Asmodeus, leader of the Sons of Satannish, disguises himself as Strange. He plans to drop in on the Ancient One, say hi to "his" master, and steal the sacred Book of the Vishanti. Somehow this means that Strange cannot return to Earth as his normal self, because his "very face and form" are already in use there. So he slaps on a mystical ski mask and proclaims: "Many can be the forms, and many the faces, of Doctor Strange!"

DOCTOR
STRANGE

12¢
IND.

177
FEB

MARVEL
COMICS
GROUP

APPROVED
BY THE
COMICS
CODE
AUTHORITY

DR. STRANGE

HAIL THE MASTER!

We're nearing the end of this run of *Doctor Strange*, so sales were probably slipping. That suggests a tactical reason for the mask: to make the character look more like a conventional super hero. The end result doesn't really hit the target, commercially or artistically.

Anyway, as Asmodeus dies, Strange unmasks him as Doctor Benton. Guess he got tired of all that charity work. Benton manages to choke out a spell releasing a pair of god-monsters from *Thor*, setting them loose in a story that continues into *Avengers* #61—another likely attempt to juice sales of *Doctor Strange*. The result feels rushed, but the *Avengers* story does include an emotional scene where Strange must operate on the wounded Black Knight, wielding a scalpel in his shaking hands for the first time since "that night."

That scene suggests, very subtly, that the damage done to Strange's hands just might be psychological in nature, rather than physical. It's a fascinating idea with deep implications for the character's origin; perhaps, hating his former life, he subconsciously robbed himself of his skill in order to force himself to change. But it's not particularly relevant to his current life, and no writer ever picks it up again.

In #180, Strange takes Clea out for New Year's Eve in Times Square. Just before midnight they run into Strange's "old friend," bestselling author/journalist Tom Wolfe.

"Haven't seen you since you were just a Kandy-Kolored, Tangerine-Flake Streamline Baby!" Strange exclaims, noting to Clea that he hasn't seen Wolfe "since '64"—the year *The Electric Kool-Aid Acid Test* was published, citing Doctor Strange.

By this time, mid-1969, that sort of attention wasn't unusual. Marvel had spread out into the larger culture, helped along by Stan's ceaseless promotional efforts. In addition to *Acid Test*, Doctor Strange had appeared on a Pink Floyd album cover and a poster for a high-profile Bay Area concert. Comics had always been part of the mix, ushered furtively into the back of the club by their youthful fans. Now they were being let in the front door.

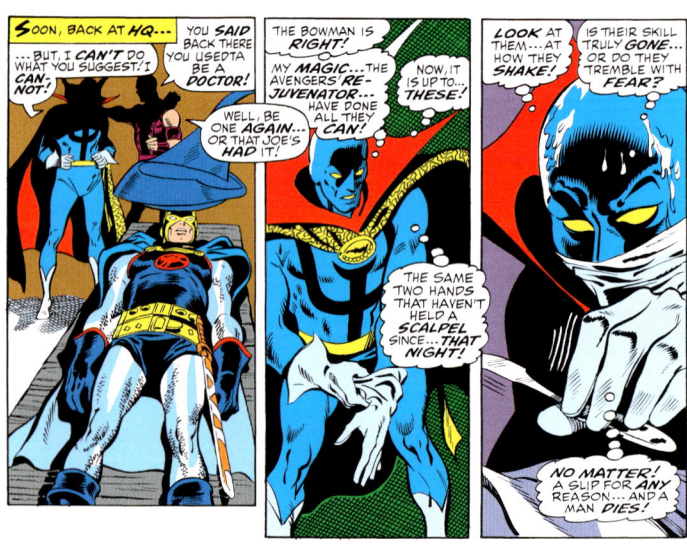

Still, we're nearing the end for *Doctor Strange.* Thomas dutifully ushers in a long line of power players, from Nightmare to Eternity to *X-Men* villain Juggernaut, pitting Strange and Clea against a time-traveling threat to all reality. Nightmare imprisons Eternity, and challenges Strange to battle "in a stygian world where one misstep—one fatal flaw in judgement—spells DEATH!!"

Colan and Palmer continue to shine, rendering otherworldly spider web pathways and snowy Manhattan nights with equal panache. But issue #179 interrupts the proceedings for a reprint, and with #181 the series drops from monthly to bi-monthly—never a good sign.

Strange continues to sport his weird new mask, on one thin pretext after another. In #178 he claims to have learned "how dangerous it is for other humans to know the identity of the mystic who walks among men." (Fans noted that this logic was shaky because "Doctor Strange" isn't a secret identity—*it's his real name.*) In #181, staring into a mirror, he hopes the mask will hide "the nagging uncertainty written large upon my brow."

In issue #182, as Wong accepts a telegram for the absent Doctor Strange, we learn at last the address of the mystic house: 177A Bleecker Street. This is a sort of primordial Easter egg, from an era before they were common: Roy Thomas lived at that address for eighteen months, along with Bill

Everett (remember him?) and, by some accounts, writer Gary Friedrich.

In July 1969, Ted Kennedy drove his car off a bridge, causing the death of a young female companion and destroying, forever, his chances of becoming President of the United States. Two days later, Neil Armstrong and Buzz Aldrin landed on the moon. And two weeks after *that, Doctor Strange* #183 materialized on the newsstands. The issue ended in mid-story; the letter column gave no indication that this was the last issue. The final caption read simply, "Next: The Searchers!"

Eras were ending, while others had barely begun.

4

1970–1972: The Flickering Flame

Pop historians often cite the Altamont, California speedway festival, in December 1969, as the spiritual end of the 1960s. The one-day event, a tumultuous concert where patrons died in car accidents and drowned in ditches, climaxed when members of the Hell's Angels security force brutally beat a man to death while Mick Jagger, on stage, pleaded for the audience to stay calm.

Exactly three months later, in New York City, another tragedy ushered in the new decade with a literal bang.

On March 6, 1970, a massive blast erupted from beneath a Greenwich Village townhouse. Two women staggered out of the smoke and dust, one of them completely nude; both were later ID'd as belonging to the Weather Underground, a radical anti-war group whose goal was nothing less than the overthrow of the United States government. Their basement bomb factory had exploded, setting off a huge supply of dynamite and killing three of their own members.

The building was gutted, ruined; smoke poured out of it for hours. Actor Dustin Hoffman was among those living next door. His wife had been speeding past in a cab at the time—if her driver hadn't missed the address, she might have been killed. What none of them knew, until much later, was the sheer quantity of dynamite being stored in that basement. "Had all the explosives detonated," an FBI report stated, "the explosion would have leveled everything on both sides of the street."

Thanks to Roy Thomas, and Wong, we now knew the location of Doctor Strange's house: seven blocks south of the blast and two blocks west. But by March, the doctor was no longer at home. Strange found himself back wandering the docks, wind shivering through him, alone and abandoned—metaphorically speaking, of course. For the first time since 1963, he had no regular feature of his own.

Thomas wasn't going to leave the character out in the cold completely. He pivoted quickly in response to *Doctor Strange's* cancellation, wrapping up his unfinished story in two other series he was writing. In *Sub-Mariner* #22 and *Incredible Hulk* #126, the two title characters find themselves temporarily yanked out of their own ongoing storylines to assist Strange against the menace of the Undying Ones.

Bill Everett's Prince Namor, the Sub-Mariner, was one of Marvel's first characters, the imperious ruler of the undersea land of Atlantis. Lee and Jack Kirby had revived him as a *Fantastic Four* villain, then spun him off into his own series. His story here is a bit of a homecoming, as artist Marie Severin returns briefly to Doctor Strange. Then it's on to the Hulk, the company's moody, hot-tempered monster. Both characters were consistently portrayed as loners during this time, rarely working with other heroes—the Hulk famously stomped away from the Avengers after a grand total of two issues.

The stories take place one after the other; though Namor and the Hulk both lend Doctor Strange a hand, the two of them never actually meet. Still, Thomas was already laying the groundwork for something new.

The last page of the Hulk story feels like an ending, if a rushed one. Strange nurses the de-Hulked Bruce Banner back to health, then tells him, "When your dizziness passes, we'll both be leaving." Pressed by Banner, he explains: "Perhaps Doctor Strange is no longer needed. Perhaps the world is ready for plain, ordinary Stephen Strange again—a former surgeon, who can still be useful as a medical consultant."

This resolution neatly sidesteps several problems. In the final issues of *Doctor Strange*, yet another confusing reality-shift had led Eternity to change Strange's name to "Stephen Sanders"; the dialogue here shows that Strange no longer has a use for the alias. Strange's words also harken back to Doctor Benton's pleas that he "give up this useless existence … and be of service to humanity again." Finally, as an Earthly doctor, Strange won't need a face-mask anymore—at least, not that one.

On a deeper level, however, this is a deliberate humbling on Strange's part. With the defeat of the Undying Ones, he forsakes a great responsibility that he sees as no longer necessary, in order to become a normal man. A well-paid man, presumably, but a mere assistant to the sort of rock-star surgeon he once was. This echoes the choice made way back in the origin story, where Strange must abandon his former fame and notoriety in favor of spiritual contemplation.

There's no mention of Clea or Wong here—but then, it's the Hulk's comic. Strange was lucky to get a guest-shot. After this, the magician does his own vanishing act; Doctor Strange will not appear in a Marvel comic for twenty months.

The company carries on, of course. A year after Strange's appearance in *Sub-Mariner*, issues #34–35 of that comic feature guest appearances by the Hulk and the Silver Surfer, a space-born Lee-Kirby character best known for his anguished philosophical monologues. Seeds are being sown, but Strange himself remains absent.

Meanwhile, in 1971, the underground Gaslight Café—one of the Village's most famous "scofflaw coffeehouses"—doused its flame after thirteen years of poetry, folk music, and late-night espresso. It would reopen fifteen years later as the Scrap Bar, a cheery, crowded, heavy-metal-themed pub that was part of my own New York experience. But that's another era, another story.

Doctor Strange didn't have to wait anywhere near that long. In late 1971, a quarterly comic called *Marvel Feature* launched with a brand-new team of heroes: The Defenders. Strange got third billing on the debut cover, beneath two now-familiar frenemies, the Hulk and Sub-Mariner. A small blurb at the bottom promised: "*Bonus!* Still another all-new blockbuster: The *Return* of Dr. Strange!"

Both stories are written by Roy Thomas; the ten-page back-feature actually takes place before the main event, so let's tackle it first. We open on Strange, dressed in street clothes with an elegant cloak over his shoulders, head bowed in thought. "A man walks alone the shadowed streets of New York's Greenwich Village," the caption tells us, "and he remembers—remembers when he was *more* than a man." Strange, who now lives "dozens of blocks from here," wonders why his wanderings have brought him here, to "this street lighted only by memories—memories of a life I have sworn to forget!?"

The Village, depicted by artists Don Heck and Frank Giacoia, has a rougher, early 1970s look to it now. Menacing figures loiter under streetlamps and glare from stoops; a stray cat hisses at Strange from atop an overflowing trash can. (A metal can.) New York's descent into crime and insolvency seems to have accelerated during our hero's absence.

Strange stumbles upon his old house, which (we learn) he closed down and had boarded up following the events of *Hulk* #126. Lost in thought, he takes a moment to realize it's now lit up and clearly inhabited. Inside he finds Wong back on the job, working for *another* Doctor Strange, who wears the full-face mask shown in the last issues of his own comic.

Dr. STRANGE *MASTER OF THE MYSTIC ARTS!*

WE PROMISED IT TO YOU EARLIER THIS SELFSAME ISSUE--- AND HERE IT *IS!* THE AWESOME TALE-- MERELY HINTED AT IN THE PRECEDING *DEFENDERS* ORIGIN -- OF HOW AND WHY MARVEL'S MAGICAL MASTER TOOK UP ONCE MORE THE CLOAK OF *WHITE MAGIC*-- OF THAT FATEFUL NIGHT WHEN HE DONNED ANEW THE MANTLE OF COSMIC RESPONSIBILITY--AND CLANDESTINE *PERIL!* THIS, THEN, IS THE LEGENDARY, LONG-UNTOLD EPIC WE CHOSE SIMPLY TO CALL ---

THE RETURN!

THE TIME IS A *NIGHT,* NOT MANY WEEKS AGO: A MAN WALKS *ALONE* THE SHADOWED STREETS OF NEW YORK'S GREENWICH VILLAGE--- AND HE *REMEMBERS*--- REMEMBERS WHEN HE WAS *MORE* THAN A MAN ---

MY NEW APARTMENT IS DOZENS OF *BLOCKS* FROM HERE -- A DIFFERENT NEIGHBORHOOD, A DIFFERENT *WORLD.*

WHY, THEN, DO I FIND MYSELF WALKING *HERE* --- DOWN THIS STREET LIGHTED ONLY BY *MEMORIES* ---

--MEMORIES OF A LIFE I HAVE SWORN TO *FORGET!?*

MYSTIC MARVEL PROUDLY PRESENTS: THE GLORIOUS *RE-BIRTH* OF ONE OF ITS MOST UNIQUE, MOST-HONORED SERIES!

STAN LEE
EDITOR
ROY THOMAS
WRITER
DON HECK
ARTIST
FRANK GIACOIA
INKER
SAM ROSEN
LETTERER

Stephen Strange, having abandoned his mystic powers, falls quickly to his doppelgänger. The Ancient One rushes to his rescue, offering to restore his power—but at a price. "Mystic mastery must not be so lightly treated," the old master warns. "I can restore your powers to you … but once assumed anew— they can nevermore be discarded!"

Dazed and semiconscious, Strange must make a fateful decision: the life of a normal man, or that of a master mage. We're not privy to his thoughts (for once!), but this is without doubt a pivotal moment in the character's life. The humility he chose must be laid aside in favor of the greater good. There are no easy answers, but in the end, he agrees to the Ancient One's terms.

Once repowered, he quickly defeats the "other" Strange, who turns out to be Mordo in disguise. Strange informs Wong that they're back in business, then stalks out into the night, clearly troubled. The final caption echoes the first: "A man walks alone the shadowed streets of New York's Greenwich Village—and he remembers—when he was *but* a man—!"

This melancholy flourish, capping off a ten-pager buried in the back of the new title, fleshes out the character in a way that only Roy Thomas has done to this point. Lee and Ditko's Doctor Strange took his work as a given, the natural duties of a hero; later writers gave only the mildest lip service to the character's weighty responsibilities. Here and elsewhere,

Thomas explores the *burden* of being the world's only defense against countless interdimensional threats. We saw it in *Doctor Strange* #174, when mystical distractions led him to ignore Clea's needs. But it's driven home even more strongly here.

And so the face-mask disappears once and for all with the imposter; the name change to "Stephen Sanders" goes away after a single mention by the Ancient One; and, of course, Strange reverses his decision to abandon magic. This is Doctor Strange taken back to basics, setting the stage for his central role in a new and very different series.

"The Day of the Defenders," in the same comic, takes place "mere days later" (or "weeks," if you believe the back-feature). Yandroth, the "Scientist Supreme" last seen in *Strange Tales*— see Chapter 3—returns, having been hit by a truck and taken, mortally injured, to a hospital. (Classic Yandroth.) That's all just sort of sad until Strange learns that Yandroth has built the Omegatron, a machine that, when triggered by his death, will "explode every nuclear stockpile on Earth."

Clearly Thomas is exploring the threat of nuclear annihilation, but is there also an echo of the Weathermen incident here? We don't actually *see* the truck that hit Yandroth—maybe he, like the 11th Street bombers, got a little too close to his own experiments instead. It doesn't really matter, because pretty soon he dies on the operating table, setting off that ominous doomsday countdown.

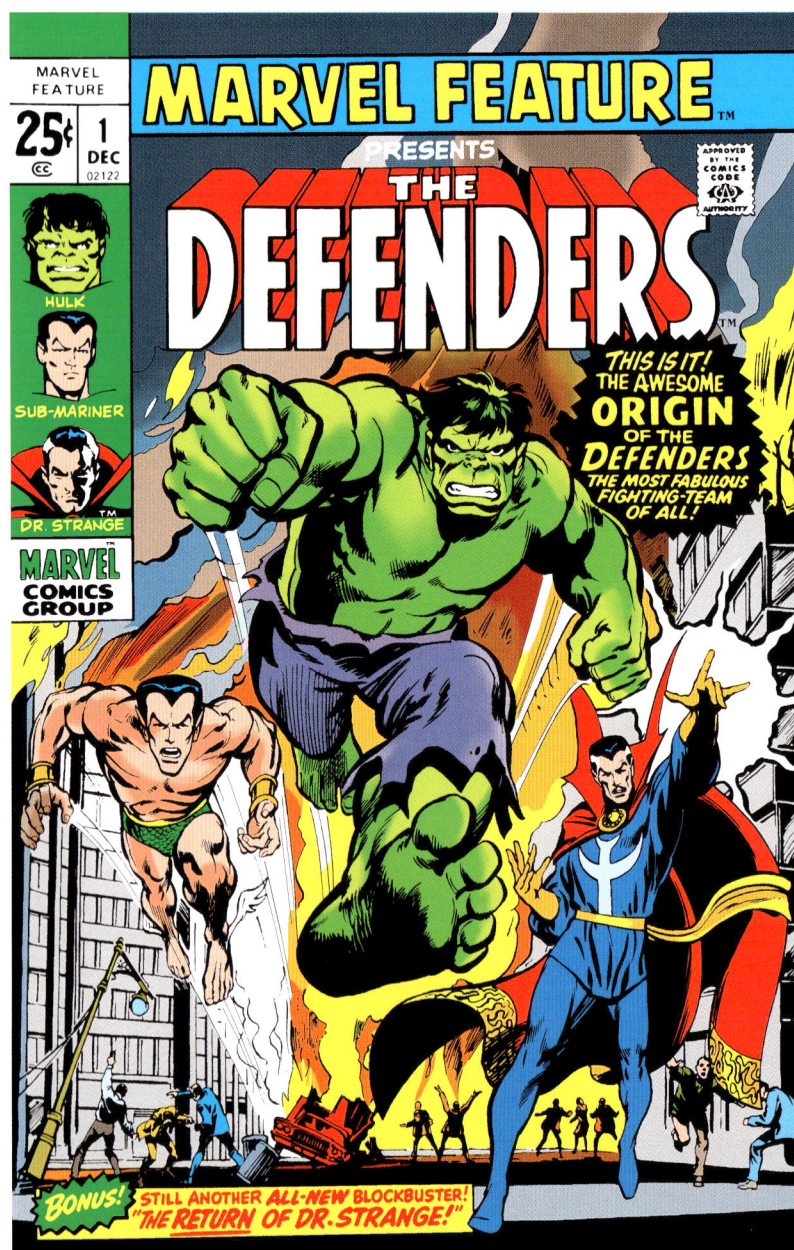

Strange, having barely settled back in his house, seeks out allies to stop the Omegatron. Namor agrees, suggesting the Silver Surfer (aha!). But the Surfer has just fallen to Earth, as men of the 1970s were wont to do. Observing him at a distance, Strange sees that he's "not badly hurt. Yet he'll not recover in time to help us—or our threatened planet." So they recruit the Hulk instead, a dicey proposition even at the best of times.

At this point we're eleven pages into a nineteen-page story, so it's straight to the Omegatron. With only seconds until it sets off the nuclear arsenals, the still unnamed Defenders find they can't destroy the machine, so Strange places it in a state of suspension where "time now passes far, far more slowly for the Omegatron than for the rest of us." This completes the nuclear fable, perhaps echoing the 1962 Cuban Missile Crisis: We've averted the catastrophe this time, but the threat still hangs over our heads.

In this and the next two issues, Thomas and his artistic collaborators pull off a rare feat: they successfully launch a brand-new super hero team. The original concept of the Defenders—a team that wasn't really a team, that only came together to face the direst possible threats—had to be modified once the group graduated to its own monthly title. But in the quarterly *Marvel Feature*, it set them apart from more formally organized teams like the Avengers and the Fantastic Four. Two of the three *Feature* stories end with the characters practically spitting about how much they hate each other. In #3, Namor declares, "Let not even Dr. Strange summon us in Earth's next hour of need … for we will not come!" The Hulk, in #1, says it even more plainly: "Hulk never wants to get together again. Never!"

In 1972, with Marvel preparing to spin off the Defenders, Doctor Strange was about to come in out of the cold. First, though, he had one more comic to drop in on, as part of his promotional tour of the Marvel Universe. To put that one in perspective, let's flash back to the mid-1960s, to the one Doctor Strange story by Lee and Ditko that we haven't discussed yet.

"The Wondrous World of Doctor Strange" headlines *Amazing Spider-Man Annual* #2 (1965), backed up by an assortment of pinups and reprints. Lee's introductory blurb, breathless as always, proclaims: "This could be called our 'be nice to Stevey Ditko' issue! We wanted to feature a really off-beat yarn for Spidey's annual, and Steverino dreamed this one up! (The fact that he also draws Doc Strange *may* have had something to do with it!)"

The story: An earthly sorcerer named Xandu wants to reassemble the powerful Wand of Watoomb. He already has half of it, but Doctor Strange has the other half locked up in his collection of mystic artifacts. So Xandu's hypnotized bruisers invade Strange's home, battling both him and Spider-Man. The final brawl is a lot of fun, with a baffled Spider-Man popping in and out of mystic portals. Strange helps him via mental suggestion and astral projection, but the two don't actually meet until page 18 (of 20).

The annual went on sale in June 1965, just as the Dormammu-Eternity conflict was heating up over in *Strange Tales*. As in those later Strange stories, Ditko receives plotting credit here. Considering the vast difference in tone and milieu between the two series, the crossover comes off remarkably smoothly. From the gorgeous splash page onward, Ditko pours a lot into the art, employing more detail than his monthly deadlines sometimes allowed.

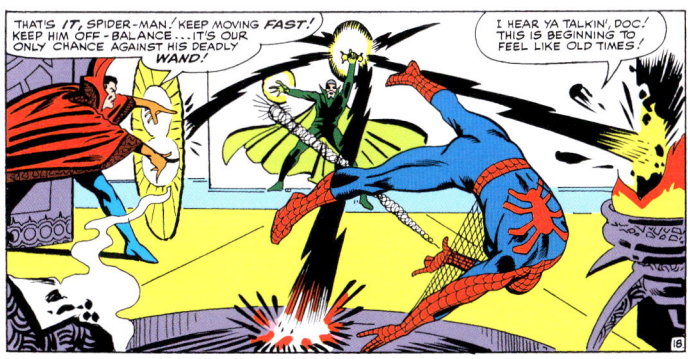

From Editor Stan's perspective, this could be seen as a promotional move as well. *Amazing Spider-Man* outsold *Strange Tales* by a considerable margin; a guest appearance by Strange in the other character's comic couldn't possibly hurt. It also fit Lee's overall strategy, to cross over the Marvel characters with each other as often as possible—creating the sense of a world of friends and common enemies, of characters who interacted with each other on a regular basis.

Just under a year later, Ditko left Marvel; we've already covered what happened to the Doctor Strange feature. On *Spider-Man*, Lee replaced Ditko with John Romita Sr., whose slick, elegant stylings and attractive character designs helped drive sales even higher.

And six years after *that*—the same month that *Marvel Feature* carried the last of the initial Defenders stories—Doctor Strange made his second visit to *Amazing Spider-Man*. Issue #109's title, "Enter: Dr. Strange!", is both simple and appropriate. Writer Stan just drops the character into the middle of a two-part story, a thriller centering on Peter Parker's high school nemesis Flash Thompson, now a troubled Vietnam veteran. Strange is already on the case when he contacts Spider-Man; he helps solve the mystery, takes Spidey where he needs to be, and then casts a spell to solve the problem. He's a virtual mystic ex machina.

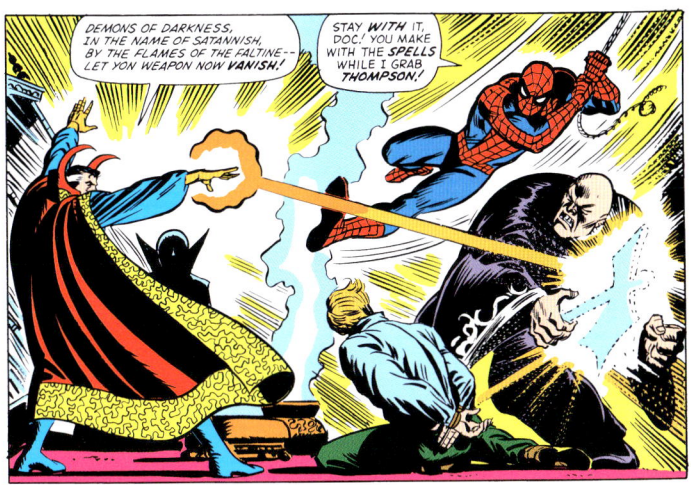

When Strange and Spider-Man greet each other, a footnote reads: "If you wonder how they know each other, they've met before! A no-prize if you remember when! ('Cause we don't!) – Stan." This clearly, if amusingly, shows how quickly the entire Marvel line has blurred across Lee's desk; he's forgotten all about the annual. It's like the old joke about the 1960s: If you remember the Marvel Age, you weren't really there.

More seriously: This is Lee's second-to-last issue of *Amazing Spider-Man*, and one of Romita's final art jobs on the title as well. As Marvel exploded in size, newly promoted Publisher Stan gave up his writing duties; he held onto *Amazing Spider-Man* and *Fantastic Four* the longest, but by 1972 he had to let them go. Romita became art director, first unofficially and then in actual title. In a way, both of them said farewell to their old 1960s haunts, turning over the mike to the hippies.

But first, in one of their last performances together, Lee and Romita parted the velvet ropes of *Amazing Spider-Man*, letting their mystic guest-star take the stage one more time. As for Writer Stan, he still had one more Doctor Strange story in him … as we'll see.

5

1972–1973: Man Nor Magic

When things started to break for Doctor Strange, they broke fast. Mid-1972 saw the launch of a regular monthly *Defenders* comic, continuing the series from *Marvel Feature*. The first issue featured Strange front and center alongside Namor and the Hulk. Writer Steve Englehart, a relatively new name at Marvel, even picked up on some plot threads from the final 1969 issues of Strange's own series.

At its launch, *Defenders* played as a super-hero team book with unusually chaotic dynamics. The group had no headquarters, no organizational structure, no real mandate except *Save-the-world-in-the-next-ten-minutes-or-it's-doomed!!* Within that context, Stephen Strange filled a new and different role. The brooding loner became a de facto den mother to the temperamental Namor and in particular to the childlike but violent Hulk.

Defenders #1 opens as Namor falls to Earth, unconscious, landing super-conveniently right in front of the Hulk. Reasoning that his friend needs medical help, Hulk leaps all the way to Greenwich Village to find Strange—the only "doctor" he knows. Like many newcomers to the city, Hulk can't handle the sensory overload. "New York!" he rages. "Hulk hates New York! Too many people! Too much noise! Bad air!"

Just wait, Hulk. Things are about to get worse.

But this is a book about Stephen Strange, not Bruce Banner—and just one month before the *Defenders* comic launched, Strange also returned to full-feature status in a comic called *Marvel Premiere*. (Not *Feature*; *Premiere*.) As previously noted, the company was expanding fast. The first *Marvel Premiere* series, a costumed religious allegory called "(The Power of) Warlock," graduated to its own comic after just two issues. That left a hole in the newly launched title, which Doctor Strange filled as of issue #3.

The 22 post-Ditko stories in *Strange Tales*, discussed in Chapter 3, only superficially resemble a single story. The Strange saga in *Marvel Premiere* #3–10 actually *is* one—but like its predecessor, it speeds along like a runaway train, shifting tones/locales/priorities with reckless speed. No fewer than six writers and twelve artists contribute to those eight issues, and that's not even counting the all-star art team called the "Crusty Bunkers," who ink the final installment.

The series starts off in a strong, if familiar, vein. *Marvel Premiere* #3's cover proclaims "HE LIVES AGAIN!!" and tells you right off: "BY STAN LEE AND BARRY SMITH." (Smith also receives plotting credit on the story; inks are by returning amulet-wielder Dan Adkins.) At the time, Marvel rarely credited creative people on its covers. DC had bannered "KIRBY IS HERE!" on a few recent comics, so this might have been a response. Or maybe Barry Smith just had enough heat from his dazzling work on *Conan the Barbarian*—see below.

Inside, "While the World Spins Mad!" (should that be "Madly"?) plays a round of familiar Strange-vs-Nightmare chords, except that this time Nightmare has been dispatched by some other, unknown force. Smith and Adkins draw a top-shelf Doctor Strange; even in a crowded story, both the city and the otherworldly scenes look masterly, effortless, a perfect balance of detail and economy. A half-page panel on page 11, where the sorcerer looks out his window to see the world transformed, is particularly luscious.

Early on, the Ancient One warns Strange: "The one who threatens you is known to me. I cannot tell you less. I cannot tell you more … His power is his secret. And his secret is his power. When you learn the one, you will face the other. If you learn it not, you will be destroyed. I can say no more." With this ominous prophecy, Lee and Smith ratchet up the stakes: We've seen the Ancient One haunted by old sins before, but we've never seen him knowingly withhold information that might get his disciple killed.

On pages 12–13, Strange beholds a twisted mirror-image of his own face in the bark of a grove of trees, echoing the Ancient One's warning. When Nightmare appears, a few pages later, he too proclaims: "My secret is my power! My power is my secret!" But with Nightmare's defeat, Doctor Strange realizes that "the true deadly foe is yet to appear." That lurking enemy remains the cohesive thread as a succession of writers cycle, musical-chairs-style, through *Marvel Premiere*.

And the music starts up right away. Issue #4, "The Spawn of Sligguth!", is credited to writer Archie Goodwin with artists Barry Smith and, in his first appearance here, Frank Brunner, with a plot credit to Roy Thomas. There's another line, too—

one that will remain for several issues to come: "Featuring concepts created by Robert E. Howard." Howard, best known as the creator of Conan, was a prolific, trailblazing pulp writer who died by his own hand at age 30, in 1936. Between 1970 and 1972, Thomas and Smith sparked the attention of fandom with their striking, comics-format adaptations and extensions of the Conan mythos, many of which featured sorcerers as villainous forces. Here we see Thomas porting that mythology over to Marvel's *other* magic-themed series.

The story that follows owes as much to H.P. Lovecraft as it does to Howard, though the two writers knew each other and used similar mythologies in their work. Such elements as the ancient tomes of power, the creepy New England town of Starkesboro, and "the mark of Sligguth—dread god of the shadowy serpent-folk of pre-cataclysmic Valusia!" show the influence of both writers. We end as a mob of cultlike townsfolk prepare to sacrifice Doctor Strange on a demonic altar, to keep him from interfering in "the waking of the Great One who Slumbers." (His secret, presumably, is his power, and his power is … well, you know.)

That cliffhanger picks up in #5 with another, completely different creative team: artists "Irv Wesley" (a pseudonym for veteran Sam Kweskin) and Don Perlin, with writer Gardner F. Fox. Fox, a skilled and popular DC writer, was best known for a defining eight-year run on the original *Justice League of*

America. Those stories featured perfect square-jawed heroes and scientific puzzle plots—everything Marvel, with its gut-punch character-oriented approach, had defined itself against. Fox had also written pulp novels in a variety of genres, including fantasy; but his style proved an uneasy match with Marvel, both here and in the other western and horror series he worked on.

We learn the name of the lurking enemy when a priestess tells Strange: "In those long-forgotten eons of Earth—in those primal days of our world's beginning—Shuma-Gorath was all … His name was whispered in reference by every living thing!" Like any good elder god, Shuma-Gorath—the name is an obscure Robert E. Howard reference—has been sleeping for millennia, while his faithful cult prepares for his return.

This issue reintroduces Clea, who tries to rescue Strange after Umar of the Dark Dimension sends her a prophetic dream—a left-field plot thread that's completely forgotten after this point. Also notable: Seeking help, Doctor Strange calls directly on the Vishanti, a hazy term for a cluster of ancient gods alluded to throughout the series, but never before shown or explained. Here the Vishanti, depicted as three beings of ambiguous cultural descent, basically tell Strange that they fought Shuma-Gorath long ago, but now it's up to him. Sorry!

Fox stays on as writer for issues #6–8 while a parade of young, cosmically inclined artists march through the pages:

Frank Brunner (on pencils this time), P. Craig Russell, and Jim Starlin, along with a police lineup of veteran inkers. Most of the fun comes from the monsters. Brunner does a great Shambler from the Sea, Russell draws nice underwater creatures, and Starlin brings a sci-fi edge to Fox's sword-wielding demons and a menacing human-flytrap hybrid.

Bits of plot, just quickly: The hastily introduced Shadowmen kidnap the Ancient One, taking him to (deep breath) the Crypts of Kaa-u the Accursed in the Lost City of Shuma-Gorath. Strange travels to yet another Creepy Rural Town, this one in the south of England. Clea and Wong try to help him, but wind up needing to be rescued themselves … I'm losing you, aren't I? Again, everyone's doing their best here, but the eldritch horror never really clicks, despite all the talk of "frightful abysses of forgotten fears and chasms of primordial horrors [that] gape wide to destroy our world!" By issue #8—the last to bear the Robert E. Howard credit—it begins to look as if an ambitious saga, begun with promise by Lee and Smith and shepherded behind the scenes by Thomas, might spell the end to another Doctor Strange series.

Fortunately, a new creative team was not only waiting in the wings, they'd already been understudying for their parts. Artist Frank Brunner had inked Barry Smith, penciled one issue himself and, by some reports, helped out on some of the later issues of the 1968 series. Writer Steve Englehart was new to the book, but as noted above, he'd been writing the character in *Defenders* for the better part of a year.

Working closely together, these creators slipped into both the character's head and his surreal milieu as if they'd been living there all their lives. Their work is filled with callbacks to previous stories, but infused with the sensibility of a younger generation. A generation shaped by folk music, rebellion, psychedelics, Beat poetry—and Doctor Strange himself.

Gardner Fox, in a bit of unintended irony, had left Strange marooned on a dead planet with no visible way home. Ditko and Lee would have had him whip out the amulet, straight off; Thomas might have thrown another complication at him, some previously unseen demon or old enemy taking advantage of his plight. Under Englehart, Strange declares: "When all else is found futile, there yet remains my inner self! Everything contains its own creation … and destruction. The flaw in Shuma-Gorath's design can be found. I have but to see it."

So he levitates into a floating lotus crouch, described here as "the position of Nirvana," and begins to meditate. The amulet rises from his neck to become a third eye on his forehead, an image first seen in *Strange Tales* #120 but rarely reprised since. With meditation comes wisdom, and with the eye comes insight; Strange locates the planet's weak spot, blows it up, and rides the shockwave out into the cosmos.

This   sequence   combines   religious   imagery,   explicit philosophy, heroic action, and mind-blowing widescreen visuals. All in less than four pages.

And we're just getting started. On his way home, Strange battles a familiar demon, chats with the still unseen Shuma-Gorath, and experiences a vision of himself, blank-eyed and crucified. "Neither man nor magic," he exclaims, "can measure these phantoms!" Brunner handles the crucifixion very delicately; you might not even recognize the imagery without Englehart's dialogue. The two of them walked a thin line with Marvel on religious themes, both here and in the following storyline. Roy Thomas and Jim Starlin, separately, explored similarly challenging themes in *Warlock* around this same time.

Back on Earth, Strange finds the Ancient One in the Crypts of Kaa-u (remember them?), guarded by the Living Buddha, who looses an army of Shadowmen on our heroes. But the real drama bubbles to the surface when the Ancient One reveals that he has *chosen* not to leave the Crypts, and is deliberately starving himself to death. Strange barely has time to process this before the Shadowmen overwhelm him.

I haven't said this at any other point, but if you want to avoid spoilers, you might want to stop here.

The Ancient One chooses to save his disciple's life, knowing that, for reasons not yet explained, this will open the gate for Shuma-Gorath to appear on Earth. Brunner and Englehart temper the Howard/Lovecraft influence; when the ancient god appears at the start of issue #10, Doctor Strange describes him as "the negative image of the Ancient One [swirling] upward from his brow!" Later in the issue, however, Shuma-Gorath assumes his "true form": a tentacled horror with a huge single eye.

But wait—what in the name of the Vishanti is going on here? Thankfully, Shuma-Gorath is as chatty an evil presence as, well, almost every other villain Doctor Strange has ever faced. "I was spawned in a dimension diametrically opposed to thine," S-G explains, "though I long since did enter this one—and I fed upon the strengths of this realm's Sorcerer Supreme, becoming his exact opposite!"

Strange fills in the gaps: Over the course of the Ancient One's 600-year lifetime, he and Shuma-Gorath have become one. The Ancient One tried to end his own life in order to destroy this menace at the same time. Released at last, Shuma-Gorath taunts Strange with visions of what is to come. Strange sees himself buried alive, followed by images of the entire human race worshiping a cult of evil. (The character experiences a lot of visions in Englehart's stories, often of himself in a state of death or distress.)

The surrealism continues as Strange enters the mind of the unconscious Ancient One. This follows directly from *Strange Tales* #137, where he probed his mentor's mind in search of the secrets of Eternity. This time, "all is spinning, surging madness!" More visions follow, of past enemies this time: Nightmare, Dormammu. The past begins to collide with the present.

We cut away to see other magicians sensing the "battle for mankind's soul": Mordo, Clea with Wong, even dear old Victoria Bentley. At last Strange comes to the only real conclusion, the one he's been trying not to face: He must kill the Ancient One.

And so he does, in a spectacular two-panel page depicting, as well, the simultaneous death of Shuma-Gorath.

In a chilling follow-up panel, Strange stands blank-eyed as the crypt walls begin to crumble around him. Having confirmed the Ancient One's death, he intones: "That means— the world is safe from Shuma-Gorath … but Dr. Strange is a murderer." He strides away, thinking: "I—who swore oaths both Hippocratic and mystical to preserve life—have killed my teacher!"

Both Hippocratic and mystical. With this single line, Englehart unites the two sides of the character, more meaningfully than any previous writer has done. Before he found enlightenment, Doctor Strange was an arrogant, selfish man; afterward, he became attuned to the greater rhythms of the universe. But through it all, as both surgeon and mage, one virtue has characterized his every action: He preserves life.

No more.

"I promised the Ancient One I would never renounce my mystic powers," he continues, referring to the events of *Marvel Feature* #1. "Yet no assassin should wield such knowledge! I shall break my promise as I broke my oaths ... I shall turn away from the occult!" But before he can make good on this resolve, the Ancient One appears to him, having graduated to a higher state of being, and implores him not to abandon magic. "You are fully worthy," the Ancient One tells him, "to become this realm's new Sorcerer Supreme." With all due humility, Strange accepts.

In many ways, this is a true and deliberate ending to the saga begun in *Strange Tales* #110, where—remember!—the Ancient One tells Strange, "my days are numbered." In issue #127 he elaborates, "It is *you* who shall replace me when the time comes for me to breathe the final vapors of Valtorr," then thinks to himself: "I pray that the awesome weight of the responsibility, and the unimaginable loneliness, will not be more than he can bear." Here, as Strange finally achieves his ascension, Englehart's closing caption tells us "the sky breathes a soft farewell ... and amid a quickening wind, Stephen Strange stands alone."

More echoes: The Ancient One's past sins, described in *Strange Tales* #148, serve as a warmup for his role as conduit and enabler to Shuma-Gorath. And after he dies, he appears to Strange as a disembodied presence in the trees and rivers all around. This evokes both the Ancient One's first, false death in *Strange Tales* #157—where he spoke his "dying" words from within a pillar of Stonehenge—and also Stephen Strange's vision of his own image in the trees from *Premiere* #3, the beginning of the current story cycle.

The assumption of the Ancient One's mantle marks the end of a journey for Strange, and the beginning of a new one. But it's not quite the end of *our* story—not yet. As a marginal character with a history of rotating creative teams, Doctor Strange still occupied a shaky spot within the Marvel Universe. In just two issues, Englehart and Brunner had taken their hero from the depths of space to the heart of his mentor's ego, killing a major character and permanently leveling up Doctor Strange's power. Now they decided to *really* swing for the fences.

First, though, they found themselves stumbling over the hard realities of periodical publishing. With issue #11, the bimonthly *Marvel Premiere* went to an awkward seven-times-a-year schedule—essentially the same six issues as before, with an extra number added in mid-summer. This took a toll on the creative team's deadlines, and issue #11 "went reprint," with pages from *Strange Tales* #115 and 117 chopped up into a combined flashback. Englehart and Brunner contribute a short framing sequence, in which Strange travels to the Ancient One's Himalayan sanctuary to tell a faithful servant of the master's death.

For a hastily concocted scene, it works surprisingly well. The splash page in particular, with Strange approaching the temple in a swirl of wind and snow, is gorgeous. Strange confesses his doubt that he can replace the Ancient One; the servant, Hamir, replies, "No one needs to, man of mystery. You will hew your own legend—your own place in the chronicles of sorcery." Brunner gives us a lovely, downcast Strange face as the mage replies: "You shame me, Hamir."

Strange orders Hamir to seal up the temple forever; its time is past. The Sorcerer Supreme will operate from his own Sanctum Sanctorum, in the heart of the new world.

But when we pick up with Strange in the following issue, he's far from that Sanctum—and still absorbing the enormity of his new station. He spends nine days meditating in the hot desert sun, floating in Nirvana position, until Wong and Clea rattle up in a jeep to drag his magic ass home. First, though, he picks up a small lizard and, marveling at the gift of life, begins to weep. When Clea joins him, we see the bond between them.

Back home, he selects her as his disciple—paying forward the honor granted him by the now-departed Ancient One.

Then he sets out to find and make peace with Baron Mordo, viewing this as an obligation conferred on him by his new position. It's also yet another natural evolution of the characters, as established nearly a decade ago. Strange winds up mesmerized—literally—by a woman with her own grudge against Mordo; she dies in battle with the Living Gargoyle (a lot of Living Whatsits floating around here). Mordo, for his part, is already gone.

Searching his enemy's chambers, Strange finds the ancient Book of Cagliostro and realizes Mordo has learned a forbidden secret: "how to change the past—without endangering one's present existence." He follows Mordo back through the timestream …

… and for the next two issues, we're treated to a constant psychedelic assault on the senses, an unstoppable raft-ride down the rushing currents of time. Strange catches up quickly with Mordo, whose dialogue reminds us that this is the first time they've met since Mordo impersonated him and took over his home. Mordo flees; Strange follows him to his destination, eighteenth-century Paris, where Strange finds a man being honored in the streets. "Cagliostro," Strange realizes. "Yes, it is he—the infamous philosopher and sorcerer!"

After a quick and futile go-around with Cagliostro, Strange disguises himself as the Parisian sorcerer, hoping to trap Mordo. But Mordo sees through the guise, and Strange soon finds himself in a disorienting time-loop: disguised as Cagliostro, facing *himself* a few minutes ago as he enters the room to find … himself.

There's a three-way battle; Cagliostro overpowers both Strange and Mordo, then reveals himself as a thirty-first-century time-traveler named Sise-Neg. He explains that the supply of mystical energy in the universe is finite, and that, in his time, three-quarters of the population use it daily. By traveling back in time to periods where fewer people wielded magic, he can absorb more of the energy himself. This accumulation of magic has caused "ripples, eddies" in the timestream, such as Doctor Strange's meeting with himself.

Eventually, Sise-Neg predicts, he will find himself alone at the beginning of time. "And what," he concludes, "is another term for an all-powerful being at the dawn of creation? … IT IS GOD!"

Mordo flies off after the sorcerer from the future: "I'll be Sis-Neg's disciple—his slave—anything—to have him recreate our era with myself as master!" Strange follows, of course, and in issue #14, the three of them hop farther and farther back through time, as Sise-Neg grows more godlike and powerful with each jump.

From this point on, the story reduces Mordo and Strange almost to observers, insects caught in the hurricane of Sise-Neg's wake. They stop off in medieval England, where Sir Lancelot mistakes Doctor Strange for Merlin (it reads cooler than it sounds), then drop in on the burning of Sodom and Gomorrah. Then it's back to prehistoric times for a surprise reunion with Shuma-Gorath, who in this era is just a plain old interdimensional monster, not yet fused with the Ancient One.

Throughout, Strange exerts the only power he has left—persuasion—by appealing to Sise-Neg's sense of mercy. Under his influence, Sise-Neg creates the Garden of Eden for the first humans to live in. Then it's even further back, to the formation of the molten Earth, and finally, inevitably, the moment before the Big Bang.

In the dark of nonexistence, Sise-Neg experiences a profound change of heart. "My plan to recreate the universe in my image was truly pitiable," he realizes. "Everything is as it should be, if one can only see it!" In showing us the futuristic sorcerer's epiphany, Englehart also displays how much more enlightened, how far ahead of his enemies, Doctor Strange has become. Just two issues ago, regarding the lizard in the desert, Strange explained: "The cosmos is everything! To affect any part of the cosmos is to affect the totality!"

He already knows.

"I shall recreate the universe," Sise-Neg declares, "exactly as it was before!" And as he lets there be light, as time turns and begins again, Sise-Neg the sorcerer becomes "the god called Genesis." (In case you hadn't figured it out yet.)

Flung back to his own time, Strange wonders: "Did we see the second creation [of the universe]—or could it have been the first, reoccurring?" He ponders Einstein and theology for a moment, but once again he's talking to himself; the experience seems to have destroyed Mordo's mind, leaving him blank-eyed and mute. When Strange notices the date, he begins to laugh: It's New Year's Day, 1974.

In that year, for the first time in history, a President of the United States resigned in disgrace. New York City's fiscal woes grew worse, leading, barely more than a year later, to a formally declared financial crisis—and President Ford's famous "drop dead" speech, denying the city federal assistance. (See, Hulk? Things got worse.)

As always, however, the bad times were good for some. *Marvel Premiere* #14 ended with this caption:

Next: The Master of the Mystic Arts in HIS OWN BOOK again! Don't miss it! (And look for an exciting NEW FEATURE in MARVEL PREMIERE!)

Englehart and Brunner had pulled off a trick worthy of a Sorcerer Supreme: catapulted a minor series to fame by catching the attention of the growing army of comic fans. And so, three months later, the newly restored universe bestowed upon its denizens an entirely new creation, something the world had never seen before: a comic book called *Doctor Strange* #1.

Another journey ended, yet another begun. Doctor Strange, in taking on the mantle and power of the Ancient One, has truly become the Sorcerer Supreme. And for his first act in that role, he has marshaled all his earthly and eldritch power to ensure the continued existence of … well, everything. Every step chronicled in this book has brought him to that point: the accident that robbed him of his surgical ability, his first reluctant lessons in sorcery, his battles with Nightmare and Dormammu, his role as a reluctant East Village celebrity, his ever-growing bond with Clea. Even the fateful decision to end his mentor's life.

(Okay, not *every* step. He probably could have done it without Yandroth.)

The saga of Doctor Strange continues, of course. But we've reached the end of the journey chronicled in these pages: from 1973 back in time, to creation and evolution, and home again. To the New York of another era, the music and poetry that built a world, through accelerating urban blight and decline and on, inevitably, to rebirth. To the rise of a Sorcerer Supreme, and the renewed flowering of the city that birthed him.

I'm no Ancient One, but I'll close with his words: "I can stay no longer! I must leave you now—forever—to pursue my new existence."

Well …

… maybe not *quite* yet.

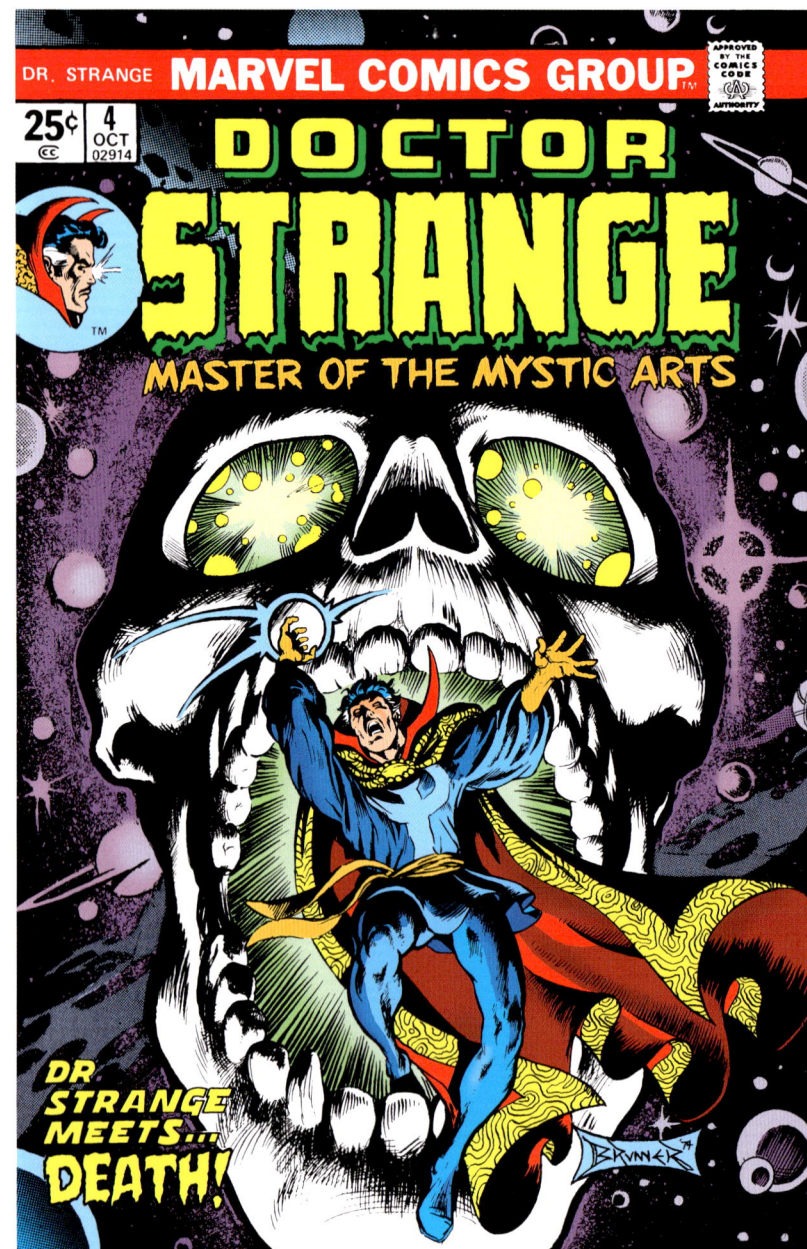

Epilogue One: Over Credits

Doctor Strange—the series—ran for an impressive 81 issues. Frank Brunner helped launch the title, then left after issue #5, to be replaced by the returning Gene Colan. Colan and Steve Englehart both departed with issue #18, succeeded by a long run of writers and artists. Since its conclusion in 1987, the series has been relaunched by Marvel several times.

The Defenders lasted even longer—a total of 152 issues in its initial run. Len Wein succeeded Steve Englehart as writer; Wein was replaced in turn by Steve Gerber, another maverick writer who altered the formula, adding new team members while keeping a strong focus on the Hulk and Doctor Strange. *The Defenders*, too, has been revived many times.

Doctor Strange—the character—went on to star in one TV movie (1978) and two theatrical films (2016, 2022) as of this writing. Total box office: $1.6 billion and counting.

Epilogue Two:
After Credits

There's an elephant in the room, if this book is a room. And it feels like a room, doesn't it? A coffeehouse, maybe, where we can all get out of the cold together. Crowd in close, listen to some poetry, talk about comics and music and high-low culture. Oh, it's getting late, isn't it? Do you have to *work* tomorrow? I forgot you had a "straight" job …

Sorry. If this book is a room, then its elephant-in-residence is the assorted conflicts among Stan Lee, Steve Ditko, and their publisher over the years. With Ditko it's a particularly tricky matter, because his priorities didn't always jibe with those of his contemporaries, and his explanations of them were often shifting and elliptical.

I can't begin to sort all that out, and this isn't the place—the *room*—to do it. What I can do is tell you about the one time, apiece, when I met Steve Ditko and Stan Lee, and maybe the time I met Doctor Strange too. The one thing about each of them that I know to be true.

Steve Ditko and Me

In the early 1990s I was working at a major comic book company—not Marvel, the other one. One of our monthly titles was based on a Steve Ditko comic from the 1970s; the new writer and artist had altered the premise significantly, remaking the series for a different time. The credits in every issue included the line: *Shade the Changing Man created by Steve Ditko.*

One day—I have no idea why—Ditko stopped into the office. Our boss, as I recall, wasn't around; I think she was on maternity leave. Ditko, whose appearance in the flesh was a rare occasion, was tall, balding, soft-spoken. He struck us as incredibly *normal*, given his reputation for eccentric sociopolitical views.

Over the course of several hours, Ditko offered his opinion on a number of subjects. The other two editors in our group engaged him in discussion; I wish I could tell you I participated, but after introducing myself, I spent most of the day editing comics. (Someone had to.) I do know that the subject of *Shade* came up. Ditko didn't fully approve of the book, but his major objection was to the credit line. He didn't believe *this* Shade was the same character he'd created.

In later issues, the line reads: *Shade is based on the character created by Steve Ditko.*

Stan Lee and Me

I worked with Stan a few times, usually long-distance. In the mid-2010s we collaborated on a series of illustrated, middle-grade prose novels. When the first one came out, we appeared at a book signing together on the crowded floor of Comic-Con San Diego.

It was a fast-moving, enthusiastic affair. Roving mobs of fans, professionals, Delta-Quadrant aliens, and would-be film producers surged past all around us. The publisher's rep told us, in no certain terms: no personalized messages. Just sign the books and move it along.

Stan, in his nineties, was as game for promotion as ever. By that time the Stan Show had become second nature to him, a good-humored act he could slip on like a sweater. He had developed some hearing trouble, though, and I soon realized part of my job was to repeat what people said into his ear. "He came all the way from Mexico to meet you!" I'd say, trying not to shout; after which Stan would turn to the visitor and say, at perfectly normal volume: "Oh, you came all the way from Mexico. That's wonderful."

At one point a reader came up and exclaimed, "This is great! I get to meet my idol!" Caught up in the Stan Show, I pointed to my collaborator and quipped, "Yeah, and him too." As I looked away, Stan backhanded me—*hard*—on the chest. I turned to him, mortally afraid that I'd offended him.

He was grinning. "Nobody likes a wise guy," he growled.

That's not the point of this story, though. After the signing was over, Stan took me by the arm. He led me to a quiet corner of the publisher's booth and leaned in.

"You wrote the book," he said.

I acknowledged that yes, I had written the book. I wasn't sure what he was getting at. Most of my contact with Stan, to this point, had been through the publisher, who had hired me. Stan and I shared credit on the book, with his name approximately twice as large as mine and as that of the artist, who had contributed dozens of beautiful full-page illustrations.

"I hate that my name's on that book," he continued, "because I didn't do it."

I assured him that I had no problem with the credit arrangement. He had created the project, and of course the publisher would want to play up his contribution. And at every stage, it had gone through his office for notes and commentary.

"Well," he said, "maybe by book three, it can be just you."

I think that's when it struck me: Nobody was listening to us. This wasn't Stan the showman, displaying his natural charm for the fans. It wasn't even the Stan who, in humbler moments, would throw around Borscht-Belt humor to casually underplay his own contributions.

I might be wrong; I wasn't inside his mind. But what I saw was a thoughtful man, a man who'd taken decades' worth of criticism to heart. A man who needed to say something to me, and to me alone.

He smiled and released my arm, like a businessman signaling that our meeting was over. His entourage closed in and, as I watched, they led him off to vanish in the crowd.

Doctor Strange and Me

On a brisk December morning way too close to Christmas, I took the subway into Manhattan to do some shopping at the Union Square holiday market. First, though, I thought I'd cruise past Stephen Strange's house in the Village. I hadn't seen the sorcerer since his pivotal appearance in my last Marvel novel, *Into the Dark Dimension.* But I still remembered the address.

I knew the neighborhood, too. A few decades ago I used to hang out at the Peculier Pub and the Scrap Bar, and feed my habit at a little place called Village Comics. (Don't look it up on Google; all you'll find is a different store with the same name that operated for a couple of years, much later.) That was a transitional time for New York, a period of recovery after the fiscal crises of the 1960s and 1970s. An uneasy bridge along the road to the tourist mecca that the city has now become.

The Doc's house looked suspiciously like a fluorescent-washed bodega, plastered with signs for beer and energy drinks. Maybe he'd cast a spell of concealment over it to discourage tourists, following the success of his recent films. I shrugged, turned up Sullivan, and paused briefly to note the Thai restaurant where Second Coming Records used to be. How long since *that* place, famous for its sprawling stacks of bootleg LPs, had been shut down by a vengeful recording industry?

I decided to swing around West 3rd to Café Reggio, one of the last survivors of the legendary Beat coffeehouses. Somehow, in all my time in New York, I'd never been to the Reggio. As I turned onto MacDougal, I did a silent-movie-style double-take.

Two doors down from the Reggio, the façade of a long-shuttered pizza parlor stood covered, roof to sidewalk, with an elaborate, glossy ad display for the Bob Dylan biopic *A Complete Unknown*. The film, scheduled to open in five days, had been shot in Jersey City on streets meticulously refitted to look just like the Village. Several of the events depicted had occurred right here on MacDougal, less than a block from where I stood. Readings and riots, music and magic, beers and brawls and hangs and happenings …

As I stared into the unnerving eyes of a larger-than-life Timothée Chalamet, I felt the shiver of a Cagliostro-style time loop. Someone had purchased this space deliberately, placed the ad *right here* on this street. Was this art imitating life? Art imitating *other* art? Art imitating art that had, in its day, sought to *express* the life of a city, a nation, at a precarious point of change?

Inside, the Reggio seemed frozen in time. Small tables, dark in the morning, sparsely occupied. Tinkle and thunder of piano music on the speakers. It reminded me of my late grandfather, a piano soloist for the Boston Pops.

I eased into a small table along the wall, between two reserved signs. A pixie-cut waitress in black, with a charming accent, brought me an oversized latte. I could almost picture her at an Allen Ginsberg reading, frowning over a flute of red wine; or maybe pushing around sets between acts at the premiere of *Little Murders*.

The world seemed to be tearing itself apart, just like in the summer of '68. But this place, this oasis of stilled time, was peaceful.

I sipped my latte, ate a messy croissant with a fork—and something odd happened. I started to notice a flicker in the corner of my eye. A fluttering, sort of a winking over by the inner wall of the café, where an ancient coffeemaker sat on display, holiday-ribboned and dark. The very machine that, per local legend, had first brought cappuccino to America, nearly a century ago.

When I glanced over, all I saw was a reflection of Christmas lights on tarnished brass. But as I turned back to my coffee, I saw it again. More than that, I *felt* it.

A sorcerer taking in the morning air, his astral form stopped in for a morning cuppa? Or old Ken Kesey's ghost hunched over in the corner, nose buried in a copy of *Strange Tales*?

I don't know. Probably neither. There's only one thing can say for sure:

It was magic.

Tamam Shud,

    Stuart Moore

P.S. I paid cash, like we used to. An offering to the ghosts.

ACKNOWLEDGMENTS

Thanks, first and foremost, to Leah Babb-Rosenfeld and Haaris Naqvi of Bloomsbury Publishing, for taking a chance on me to help launch this ambitious, wonderful line of books, and for guiding me through uncharted territory. Thanks, as well, to Zeba Talkhani, Gemma Boxal, and Kathy Daneman.

As always, thanks also to Sven Larsen, Jeff Youngquist, Jeremy West, and Sarah Singer of Marvel. Like Wolverine, they're simply the best at what they do—and a hell of a nice bunch of people, too.

Liz Sonneborn, my wife and partner, helped even more than usual. As the author of more than a hundred nonfiction books, she truly served as Sorcerer Supreme to this wide-eyed, fiction-writing naïf from the Dark Dimension.

I was stunned to learn that, of the other writers launching this series, two are friends and all three are people whose work I admire! A fierce pack of wolves to prowl the landscape with; let's do it again, folks.

A special mention goes out to the Grand Comics Database (comics.org), an invaluable source of reference for quick questions like, "Did Gene Colan draw that cover, or was it Barry Smith?" Comichron (comichron.com) also provided crucial sales figures and other statistical information. All errors, of course, are mine and mine alone.

Finally, and at the risk of being obvious, none of this would have been possible without the wonderful legacy of comics left behind by Doctor Strange's brilliant, eldritch brain trust. So a profound, grateful thank-you goes out to Stan, Steve, Roy, Dan, Gene, Tom, the other Steve, Frank—and everyone else who laid pen, pencil, or typewriter keys to paper, to conjure the magic from nothing at all.

ILLUSTRATIONS

BIBLIOGRAPHY

The Sacred Texts

Marvel has collected the works discussed here in several forms:

Marvel Masterworks: Doctor Strange Volumes 1–5
  Elegant hardcover collections.
Mighty Marvel Masterworks: Doctor Strange Volumes 1–3
  Affordable paperback editions.
Doctor Strange Epic Collection: *Master of the Mystic Arts; I, Dormammu; A Separate Reality*
  Thick paperback collections.
Doctor Strange Omnibus Volumes 1–2
Doctor Strange: Master of the Mystic Arts Omnibus Volume 1
  Large, comprehensive hardcover editions.
Marvel Unlimited (app)
  Full digital archive.

The Lesser Books of the Vishanti

The following volumes were consulted in the preparation of this book:

Bell, Blake. *Strange and Stranger: The World of Steve Ditko*. Fantagraphics, 2008.
Currie, David. *Ditko Shrugged: The Uncompromising Life of the Artist/Creator of Spider-Man and the Rise of Marvel Comics*. Hermes Press, 2020.
Delany, Samuel R. *The Motion of Light in Water: Sex and Science Fiction*

Writing in the East Village. Arbor House, 1988; Open Road Media, 2014.

Ditko, Steve. *The Complete Four-Page Series and Other Essays.* SD Publishing, 2020.

Howe, Sean. *Marvel Comics: The Untold Story.* Harper, 2012.

Kruse, Zac. *Mysterious Travelers: Steve Ditko and the Search for a New Liberal Identity.* University Press of Mississippi, 2021.

Wood, Susan. *The Best of Susan Wood.* Jerry Kaufman, 1982.

Yoe, Craig. *The Creativity of Ditko.* IDW Publishing/Yoe Books, 2012.

Scrolls and Fragments

Also consulted:

Bubbins, Harry, "When the Weathermen Blew Up 18 West 11th Street," Off the Grid, March 6, 2019, https://www.villagepreservation. org/2019/03/06/when-the-weathermen-blew-up-18-west-11th-street/.

"Café Reggio: Greenwich Village's Oldest Café Has Served up Espresso and Italian Pastries Since 1927," *New York*, accessed December 24, 2024, https://nymag.com/listings/restaurant/caffe-reggio/.

Cronin, Brian, "50 Years Ago, Dr. Strange's Creative Team Pulled a Hoax to Protect a Controversial Tale," CBR, December 31, 2013, https:// www.cbr.com/doctor-strange-siseneg-hoax-englehart-brunner-stan-lee/.

Cronin, Brian, "What's the Origin of Dr. Strange's Address?", CBR, November 14, 2016, https://www.cbr.com/whats-the-origin-of-dr-stranges-address/.

Gray, Christopher, "Good Addresses, Circa 1830," *New York Times*, December 15, 2011, https://www.nytimes.com/2011/12/18/realestate/ south-village-streetscapes-good-addresses-circa-1830.html.

"Greenwich Village, 1960s" (promotional film), YouTube, accessed December 24, 2024, https://www.youtube.com/ watch?v=RN6BdzaFiQc.

"Greenwich Village 1964. New York, the Neighborhood, a Political, Cultural Revolution," YouTube, accessed December 24, 2024, https://youtube.com/watch?v=CzsKKwuGan8.

"Greenwich Village Sunday" (short film), accessed December 24, 2024, https://archive.org/details/Greenwic1960.

Gussow, Mel, "The House on West 11th Street," *New York Times*, March 5, 2000, https://www.nytimes.com/2000/03/05/nyregion/the-house-on-west-11th-street.html.

"History", The Up and Up, accessed December 24, 2024, https://www.upandupnyc.com/history.

"The Home of the Beer," Peculier Pub, accessed December 24, 2024, http://www.peculierpub.com/#/history.

Houtman, Ben, "Mayor v. MacDougal Street," WNYC.org, February 25, 2016, https://www.wnyc.org/story/mayor-v-macdougal-street/.

Hultkrans, Andrew. "Steve Ditko's Hands." In *Give Our Regards to the Atomsmashers!,* edited by Sean Howe. Pantheon Books, 2004.

Maheras, Russ, "Steve Ditko: Inside his Studio Sanctum Sanctorum," Pop Culture Squad, March 16, 2019, https://popculturesquad.com/2019/03/16/steve-ditko-inside-his-studio-sanatorium/.

Miller, Matt, "New York's Greenwich Village in the '60s: The Photos," *Esquire*, December 21, 2017, https://www.esquire.com/entertainment/g14473188/new-york-greenwich-village-1960s-photos/.

"Murdock and Marvel: 1968," Comics Over Time, March 5, 2024, https://comicsovertime.podbean.com/e/murdock-marvel-1968/.

Nevius, James, "Bleecker Street's Evolution from Sleepy Suburb to America's Left Bank," Curbed New York, December 19, 2014, https://ny.curbed.com/2014/12/19/10009788/bleecker-streets-evolution-from-sleepy-suburb-to-americas-left-bank.

"The Numbers: Box Office History for Doctor Strange Movies," The Numbers, accessed March 31, 2025, https://www.the-numbers.com/movies/franchise/Doctor-Strange#tab=summary.

Reid, Britt, "Tom Wolfe (1931–2018) and Doctor Strange," Atomic Kommie Comics, May 15, 2018, https://atocom.blogspot.com/2018/05/tom-wolfe-1931-2018-and-doctor-strange.html.

Robinson, Douglas, "Townhouse Razed by Blast and Fire; Man's Body Found," *New York Times,* March 7, 1970, https://www.nytimes.

com/1970/03/07/archives/townhouse-razed-by-blast-and-fire-mans-body-found-explosions-and.html.

Robinson, Douglas, "Bombs, Dynamite and Woman's Body Found in Ruins of 11th Street Townhouse," *New York Times,* March 11, 1970,   https://www.nytimes.com/1970/03/11/archives/bombs-dynamite-and-womans-body-found-in-ruins-of-11th-st-townhouse.html?searchResultPosition=1

Sheryl, "Upstairs/Downstairs: A Night Out on MacDougal Street," Off the Grid, January 22, 2014, https://www.villagepreservation.org/2014/01/22/upstairsdownstairs-a-night-out-on-macdougal-street/.

"Smog Almost Killed New York City, Here's How" (short film), YouTube, accessed December 24, 2024, https://www.youtube.com/watch?v=cTQDJy0opaM.

Vassalo, Dr. Michael J., "Venus Vol. 2: A Re-Introduction." In *Venus Vol. 2: Atlas Comics Library No. 2.* Fantagraphics, 2023.

Vassalo, Dr. Michael J., "Welcome to Adventures into Terror Vol. 1." In *Adventures into Terror Vol. 1: Atlas Comics Library No. 1.* Fantagraphics, 2023.

ABOUT THE AUTHOR

Stuart Moore is a writer, a book editor, and an award-winning comics editor. Recent works include *Captain America for Dummies*; *Toxie Team-Up*, featuring the Toxic Avenger; and the original graphic novel *Meat*. Novels include three volumes of the *New York Times* bestselling series *The Zodiac Legacy*, cowritten with Stan Lee; Marvel's *Into the Dark Dimension*, *Target: Kree*, and *Thanos: Death Sentence*; and *John Carter: The Movie Novelization*.

Stuart's comics include the original sci-fi series *Captain Ginger*, *Highball*, and *EGOs*, as well as *Namor*, *Deadpool the Duck*, and *Firestorm*. Other writing includes prose and comics set in the universes of *Stargate*, *The Transformers*, *Conan the Barbarian*, *Redwall*, and *Star Trek*. At DC Entertainment, Stuart was a founding editor of both the Vertigo and Helix imprints. He has been a book editor at St. Martin's Press, editor of the SyFy Channel/Virgin Comics and Marvel Knights comics imprints, and freelance Ops director of AHOY Comics.

Stuart can be found on Facebook at stuartmoore1; on Instagram at stuartmoore01; on Bluesky at stuartmoore.bsky.social; and at stuartmoorewriter.com. He lives in Brooklyn, New York.

MARVEL AGE OF COMICS

Explore the series!

www.bloomsbury.com/marvel-books

The Mighty Avengers vs. the 1970s
by Paul Cornell

The Avengers was **the** comic book of the 1970s. From Civil Rights to Women's Lib, battles for the soul of America became battles between super heroes.

Daredevil: Born Again
by Chris Ryall

A smart, meticulous look into the compelling and original storyline of *Daredevil: Born Again*, its gorgeous and unique artwork, and its overall influence in the decades since its release.

Spider-Man: Miles Morales
by Ytasha L. Womack

A look at the hugely successful reimagining of one of the most popular super hero characters of all time.